INFORMAL READING–THINKING INVENTORY

AN INFORMAL READING INVENTORY (IRI)

WITH OPTIONS FOR ASSESSING ADDITIONAL ELEMENTS

OF HIGHER-ORDER LITERACY

ANTHONY V. MANZO

California State University, Fullerton

ULA C. MANZO

California State University, Fullerton

MICHAEL C. McKENNA

Georgia Southern University

THOMSON

WADSWORTH

Australia • Canada • Mexico • Singapore • Spain • United Kingdom • United States

Publisher	Ted Buchholz
Acquisitions Editor	Jo-Anne Weaver
Developmental Editor	Tracy Napper
Project Editor	Annelies Schlickenrieder
Production Manager	Jane Tyndall Ponceti
Art Director	Peggy Young
Composition	Norman Haskell

ISBN: 0-15-500956-7

Library of Congress Catalog Card Number: 94-76896

Wadsworth/Thomson Learning
10 Davis Drive
Belmont CA 94002-3098
USA

For information about our products, contact us:
Thomson Learning Academic Resource Center
1-800-423-0563
http://www.wadsworth.com

For permission to use material from this text, contact us by
Web: http://www.thomsonrights.com
Fax: 1-800-730-2215
Phone: 1-800-730-2214

Printed in the United States of America
10 9 8 7 6 5

PREFACE

The *Informal Reading–Thinking Inventory* breaks new ground in the area of literacy assessment. It is like most informal reading inventories in many ways; for example, it permits the examiner to assess a student's listening level, oral reading of words in isolation and in context, and basic comprehension of text. These allow an instructor to ascertain a student's relative capacity to read, level of proficiency in word recognition and analysis, and reading comprehension at the literal and certain lower levels of inference.

The *Informal Reading–Thinking Inventory*, however, actually increases the flexibility of a traditional informal reading inventory by offering options that enhance assessment beyond these typical factors. The most important of these options is a separate means of assessing student reading and thinking "beyond the lines." This is done by asking questions that require connecting what is read to prior knowledge, experience, and learning. Another option permits evaluation of the student's level of engagement with, or orientation and commitment in, addressing the test tasks. This is inferred from how well the student answers questions "congruently," rather than just correctly or incorrectly. Congruency here simply means responses that are contextually sensible, indicating that the student is engaged and intentionally listening, and not just hearing. Other options include a measure of the student's ability to evaluate his or her own comprehension, or *metacognition,* and opportunities to write in response to reading.

Why the need for these options? The *Informal Reading–Thinking Inventory* was constructed from the start to address some of the technical psychometric issues that have plagued informal reading inventories for five decades, such as intermixing passage dependent and independent questions. This inventory attempts to be responsive to the new issues that have arisen from recent theories of comprehension and philosophies of instruction, including the "constructivist" ideal of constructing a reasonable interpretation of what one reads. Also, the current movement in education toward alternative forms of assessment entails reduced emphasis on product measures, such as standardized tests, and a greater focus on "process" measures, or performance-based and diagnostic evaluation of the student's thinking, reflection, and strategy choices. Simply put, the *Informal Reading–Thinking Inventory* attempts to better assess the thinking, or meaning-making, aspects of reading that are emphasized in current views of the reading process. The expectation is that a means of *measuring* this dimension of reading will support more widespread professional discussion of, and teaching toward, these higher-order objectives.

A caveat is needed here: although this inventory has been in development for over ten years, its evolution will continue. Further developments will be guided by what you learn, think, experience, and subsequently suggest. We encourage you to write, phone, or fax us with your thoughts.

We would like to extend a special thanks to Siriwan Ratanakarn and Brenda Anderson, graduate assistants, for their considerable help in the development of this instrument. Thanks, too, to the many classroom teachers who did field evaluations; to the reviewers of the inventory—Phyllis Fantauzzo, Rider College; Edward Poostay, Bloomsburg University of Pennsylvania; Leo Schell, Kansas State University; and Carmelita Williams, Norfolk State University; and to Jo-Anne Weaver, Senior Acquisitions Editor, and Tracy Napper, Developmental Editor at Harcourt Brace, for making this publication possible.

GRAPHIC OVERVIEW

of the IR–TI

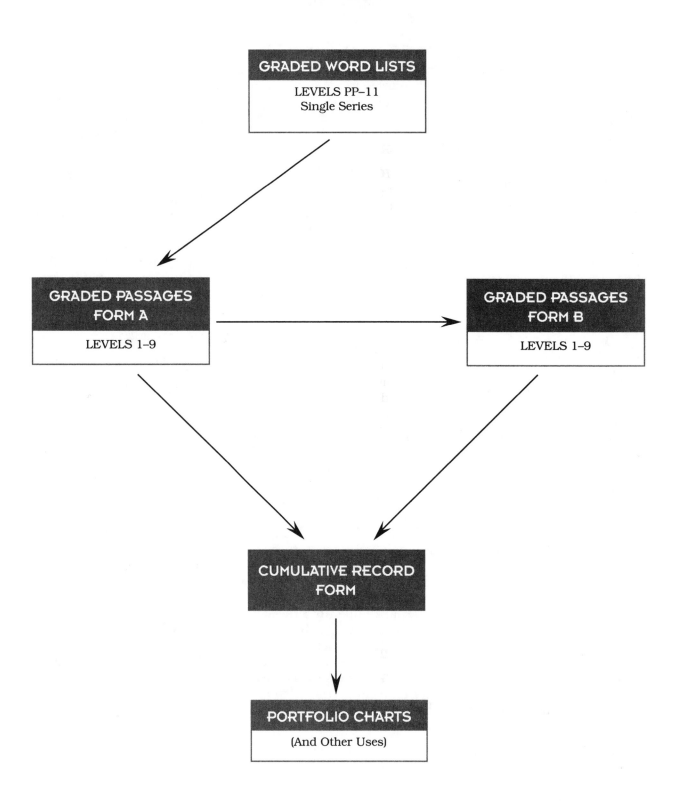

GRADED WORD LISTS

LEVELS PP–11
Single Series

GRADED PASSAGES FORM A

LEVELS 1–9

GRADED PASSAGES FORM B

LEVELS 1–9

CUMULATIVE RECORD FORM

PORTFOLIO CHARTS

(And Other Uses)

TABLE OF CONTENTS

1

MANUAL FOR ADMINISTERING AND INTERPRETING THE IR-TI

The examiner pipes and the teacher must dance—and the examiner sticks to the old tune. If educational reformers really wish the dance altered they must turn their attention from the dancers to the musicians

—H. G. Wells, 1892

SECTION 1 INTRODUCTION TO THE IR-TI

The IR-TI and Recent Developments in Assessment

A new wave in assessment is spreading across the nation. It is called "performance-based assessment," and it emphasizes determining whether students can do the complex, integrated tasks that life and learning really require rather than merely give correct answers to literal-level questions on standardized tests. In practical terms, this means that teachers should be doing more of the following:

- Offering children authentic and challenging tasks to do, such as writing a student handbook for children new to the classroom or school

- Assessing student progress as a seamless part of the tasks children are engaged in, tasks such as portfolio construction and analysis (described in more detail ahead)

- Using assessment dynamically to guide instruction, not merely for evaluation of student achievement

- Appraising higher levels of learning, such as the application and evaluation of what is read and taught

The Informal Reading–Thinking Inventory (IR-TI) is designed to help the teacher acquire further "know-how" for undertaking this seamless and dynamic type of assessment. While it does require stopping to administer the inventory initially, one of its primary purposes is to help teachers build the experiences, insights, and skills necessary to continually appraise student progress in the materials they read in more typical and authentic learning situations.

The formula for this basic instrument has been in the reading teacher's repertoire for many years. We have merely enhanced it to better orient the teacher's attention to modern conceptions of the reading process, especially the need to foster higher levels of reading/thinking in all students. It is seldom recognized, but this need is greatest in remedial level readers, who often are systematically deprived of the uplifting benefits to self-concept, motivation, and learning that come from being challenged to higher levels of thought and analysis.

One of the chief values of the IR-TI is to help you, the teacher, to personalize the question types, formats, and formulas for estimating student progress while you are engaged in teaching and discussions with your students. Ideally, as you do so, your students will begin to ask similar questions of you, of one another, and also of themselves while they read. Evidence that this actually happens is mounting quickly, as you will learn if you read the historical background section ahead. If you are primarily a hands-on learner, you may wish to skip ahead for now to the description of the instrument and its administration. No matter which order you choose, set your sights on becoming a more astute watcher of students in teaching/learning situations, for this is the basis of the superior intuition and ability needed to do seamless teaching and assessment. Seamless teaching and assessment also is known in the literature by names such as "dynamic assessment" (Cioffi & Carney, 1983) and "intervention assessment" (Paratore & Indrisano, 1987) and even much earlier as "diagnostic-teaching" (Betts, 1936). By any name, the meaning is the same: getting to know individual strengths and weaknesses so instruction can be sensibly organized to take advantage of strengths or to support areas of weakness. A basic example of this practice would be to have a weak reader first listen to some portion of a passage before reading the remainder silently.

Historical Background of the IR-TI

Near the turn of the century, E.L. Thorndike concluded from his research that "reading is reasoning" (1917). However, over fifty years had to pass before Stauffer's (1969) Directed Reading–Thinking Activity added a clear thinking component to traditional Directed Reading Activity lessons (Betts, 1946). Even with this progress, assessment of reading has remained essentially stalled at the literal to inferential levels, with little attention to the constructive nature of the reading process. The most notable attempts during this period to do more have centered around informal—as opposed to conventional standardized—testing. However, even these attempts have largely been focused on means to better analyze and interpret oral reading "miscues," as Goodman (1973) called deviations from the printed page that previously had been referred to as "errors."

This shortfall in assessment has tended to inhibit teachers and education in general from better understanding and addressing higher levels of comprehension. Attention to higher levels of comprehension will help you discover things about teaching and learning that most teachers sense but have had difficulty documenting. For example, most teachers notice that even weaker readers, such as those with erratic word calling and weak literal comprehension, often have surprising *strengths* in critical and creative thinking. The IR-TI provides a means of assessing and documenting such strengths. It also provides concrete evidence that some seemingly proficient readers have *weaknesses* that need attention. Some children, for example, have effective strategies for word recognition and literal comprehension but do not seem to connect the text to life experience or to think critically and creatively about what they read. Our inability as educators to document higher-order thinking has made it difficult for us to build on children's strengths and to remediate their weaknesses at this level. This is especially unfortunate, since emphasizing critical and creative thinking or "teaching up," as Estes (1991) refers to it, can positively benefit basic reading, writing, and thinking of students at all levels of proficiency (Collins, 1991; Cooter & Flynt, 1986; Haggard, 1976). In short, current assessment systems leave typical remedial students and those who may appear proficient, but are not, poorly served, because their needs are not documented and hence go unattended.

Why a New Type of IRI?

Since their formal origin half a century ago (Betts, 1946; Kilgallon, 1942), Informal Reading Inventories (IRIs) have become the method of choice for estimating reading and listening levels and for quickly assembling baseline information about word recognition abilities (Dechant, 1981; Johns, 1977; Lipson & Wixson, 1991). Despite their usefulness and popularity, as evidenced by numerous commercially successful instruments, a number of technical measurement issues remain inadequately addressed by IRI developers (Baumann, 1988; Searles, 1988). These include problems such as weak reliability, inadequate estimates of the difficulty levels of passages, and intermixing of passage dependent and independent questions. Thus, IRIs continue to involve something of an approach-avoidance, love-hate struggle for many educators.

Three principal facts encourage us to believe that a new kind of Informal Reading Inventory can address a number of these and other emerging assessment issues and, more importantly, can result in better decisions in planning instruction. First, the IR-TI was constructed from the start to address some of the technical psychometric issues that have plagued IRIs for five decades. For example, you will see later how we were able to solve the problem of intermixing passage dependent and independent questions rather easily with a design modification that essentially separates the two question types. A second related point is that the IR-TI attempts to be responsive to the new issues that have arisen from recent theories of comprehension and from philosophies of instruction. Chief among these new concerns is the distinction between *reconstructing* an author's intended meaning (the usual view of comprehension) and the "constructivist" concept of *constructing* a reasonable interpretation of what one reads. The IR-TI is designed to assess both of these dimensions of comprehension in a manner that grounds it in current theory by acknowledging the "constructivist" ideal of promoting higher-order literacy or literate responses. Third, the movement toward alternative forms of assessment entails reduced emphasis on product measures, such as standardized tests, and greater focus on "process" measures, or performance-based and diagnostic evaluation of the student's thinking, reflection, and strategy choices. Instead of teachers continuing the practice of not assessing at all what cannot be assessed easily and definitively, we urge teachers to use the IR-TI to become more expert in continuing to informally assess critical/creative reading and thinking in a variety of settings and classroom situations. This, again, is the basis of "performance-based" assessment.

Other Additions to the Mix

As stated above, the Informal Reading–Thinking Inventory includes the traditional components of the IRI and extends this format to include assessment of several aspects of critical/creative, or constructive, thinking. However, it also offers means for inferring aspects of attitude, language proficiency, personal-social adjustment, and learning style—factors that the examiner can further appraise with other collateral instruments, including some available at little or no cost (see "Appendix A: Collateral Instruments"). The value of this more *holistic* assessment of student progress is that it achieves a better fit with current views of the reading process, of child development, of curriculum design, and of efforts to promote greater teacher empowerment.

Hence, typical uses of the IR-TI might include:

- Guiding students into materials from which they are most likely to profit

- Assessing, reporting, and addressing individual needs

- Acquiring a richer basis for forming cooperative and needs-based groups

- Assessing largely unacknowledged strengths and deficits in selected areas of reading/ thinking (as specified later)

- Evaluating student progress in ways that more closely parallel the larger objectives of education and the modern views of the reading process

- Providing self-educating experiences for teachers in learning how to do performance- based assessment in reading/thinking

- Conducting site-based action research and program evaluation

SECTION 2 PURPOSES AND COMPONENTS

The IR-TI allows you to accomplish all of the purposes of the traditional IRI and more. The option of how to use the IR-TI always rests with you, the teacher. It can be used in exactly the same way an IRI is used (which we call the streamlined option) or it can be used to reach additional conclusions (the regular option).

Purposes of a Traditional IRI

A traditional IRI is given to determine one or more of the following:

1. Independent Level (highest level at which comprehension is good *without help*)

2. Instructional Level (highest level at which comprehension is good *with help*)

3. Frustration Level (lowest level at which comprehension is poor *even with help*)

4. Listening Level (highest level at which comprehension is good when passages are read aloud to the student by the teacher)

5. Decoding strategies used by the reader (inferred from oral reading performance)

6. Reading rate

Successful administration of a traditional IRI leads to a revealing portrait of the child as a reader. Such a portrait is based on a few logical assumptions about the graded passages the child has read or listened to. For example, the Independent Level should be lower than the Instructional Level, which in turn should be lower than the Frustration Level. A given child might have an Independent Level of second grade, an Instructional Level of third grade, and a Frustration Level of fourth grade. The Listening Level is generally at least as high as the Instructional Level, and (especially for elementary-age children) it is frequently higher. For example, it would not be surprising for this child to have a Listening Level of fourth or fifth grade. When the child is then asked to read passages aloud, the types of errors (called *miscues*) that have been made by the child can lead to insights into how the child approaches the task of word recognition. A teacher may discern, for instance, a tendency to rely too heavily on context or a habit of skipping over unfamiliar words.

Even though the creators of an IRI offer guidelines for its use, the teacher is fully empowered to modify it to suit individual needs. For example, a teacher interested primarily in placing a child into instructional materials would probably not bother determining the Listening Level or conducting an analysis of miscues. Understandably, this sort of flexibility has had great appeal for IRI users.

Purposes of the IR-TI

The IR-TI actually increases the flexibility of a traditional IRI. If a teacher wishes, the IR-TI can be used exactly like an IRI to provide the six types of information just listed and no more. This *streamlined option* has much to offer, for the information it provides is highly important. However, the IR-TI positions the teacher to discover much more about a child's reading and language development through the *regular option*. It requires asking more questions and making more judgments after each passage is read by the child, but the advantages are considerable. The IR-TI breaks new ground in the area of literacy assessment. In addition to the six types of information produced by a traditional IRI, several more types can be gathered through the IR-TI (continued here with the seventh):

7. Measurement of two dimensions of comprehension:

   • reconstructive (literal plus inferential comprehension)

   • constructive (critical and creative comprehension)

8. The degree of "engagement," or attention, in listening and responding to questions (this is inferred from a count of congruent, or relevant though not necessarily "correct," responses to questions, a notion that is more fully explained and illustrated later)

9. The extent of metacognition, as inferred from observations of self-monitoring and from quantitative counts of self-evaluations of accuracy in answering questions

10. Language development, as informally approximated from a comparison and summation of reading, listening, speaking, and writing

11. Aspects of cognitive style, as approximated from comparison of performance on the different question types

Components of the IR-TI

Like many traditional IRIs, the IR-TI is made up of a set of graded word lists and two sets of reading passages. The word lists range from preprimer to grade 11 and are used primarily to make an initial estimate of the student's reading level. This estimated grade placement then can be used to determine the level at which to begin further testing with the reading passages. The IR-TI's two sets of passages, ranging from first through ninth grade can be used to assess the student's oral and silent reading comprehension and listening capacity. They also can be used to further assess silent reading comprehension or to evaluate student progress at some later date. Figure 2-1 outlines these components for quick reference, together with passage titles.

FIGURE 2-1 IR-TI Components

Word Lists	Form A Passages	Form B Passages
PP	——	——
P	——	——
1	Alexander Calder	A Better Way
2	The Crab and His Mother	The Fox and the Lion
3	The Desert: What Lives There	Kites in Flight
4	The Fox and the Crow	The Shepherd Boy and the Wolf
5	The Big Wave	Signals and Messages
6	The Frogs Who Wanted a King	The Old Woman and the Doctor
7	Whaling	The Creation of the Sun and the Moon
8	The Cobbler Turned Doctor	The Vain Jackdaw
9	James Houston: Tales of the Far North	Awaiting the Match
10	——	——
11	——	——

Each reading passage is accompanied by a series of questions at literal and inferential levels, as on a traditional IRI. These are described as "Reading the Lines" and "Reading Between the Lines," respectively. In addition, each IR-TI passage includes questions designed to estimate the student's "Reading Beyond the Lines," or self-evaluative (or metacognitive) and constructive (critical/creative) thinking processes. Question types are not identical for each passage but are matched to the content, so they are as meaningful and authentic as these can be in a given testing situation. Figure 2-2 provides a brief description of the types of questions that might be used with any given passage. In general, questions can be broadly grouped into three categories: *reconstructive* ("reading the lines" and "reading between the lines"), *constructive* ("reading beyond the lines," or conjectural), and *metacognitive* (self-monitoring, or "reading oneself").

FIGURE 2-2   IR-TI Question Types

Familiarity and Interest

(PK)   *Prior Knowledge:* extent of familiarity with ideas or information in the text

(EJ)   *Enjoyment:* extent to which the student enjoyed the passage (affective response)

Literal ("Reading the Lines")

(F)   *Factual:* recalling information from the text

(FK)   *Fund of Knowledge:* relating the text to prior knowledge (includes some vocabulary words that cannot be defined from context)

(V)   *Vocabulary:* deriving word meanings from context

Inferential ("Reading Between the Lines")

(I)   *Inference:* logically combining facts available in the text (this level of inferencing should require very little, if any, conjecture, but it may assume a great deal of prior knowledge; e.g., a reference to a ball being struck on a golf course is expected to produce an image of a hard, small ball as opposed to all other possibilities)

Critical/Creative ("Reading Beyond the Lines")

(AC) *Abstract Concept:* extracting an essential idea

(AR) *Analogical Reasoning:* seeing or drawing meaning and insights from parallel facts or situations

(CBF) *Concept-Based Facts:* recognizing facts found in the text but that require a richer schema to understand

(CE) *Critical-Evaluative:* making judgments based on analysis of the text, possible background information, and related personal insights, experience, and/or feelings

(EX) *Explanation:* verifying and justifying

(OE) *Open-Ended Questions:* exploring relevant thoughts and ideas suggested by the passage though not stated or implied (these questions tend to offer a qualitative look at language proficiency, personal-social adjustment, and character)

(PS) *Problem Solving:* synthesizing information from textual and nontextual sources

(SC) *Schema Connection:* connecting concepts or facts from background knowledge (as in the inference example of a ball being struck on a golf course), and development of a world view

Self-Evaluative ("Reading Oneself")

(M) *Metacognitive:* self-monitoring, self-appraisal, self-correction, and self-regulation (aspects of introspection)

Grade Range Served by the IR-TI

The IR-TI is apt to be most useful with children from grades 3 through 7. While the IR-TI word lists range from preprimer to grade 11 and its passages extend from grade 1 to grade 9, its most reliable range is more modest. Like its predecessors, the IR-TI tends to be less reliable and accurate at the upper and lower extremes of the available levels. Use of any IRI with first-grade students has long been troublesome because of the likelihood that a child's independent and/or instructional levels may not exist yet. Likewise, upper IRI levels tend to involve an increasing lack of distinction between adjacent levels, both for passages and word lists.

SECTION 3 HOW THE IR-TI WAS DEVELOPED

Our goal has been to create an instrument that (1) preserves the best qualities of the traditional IRI, (2) eliminates some of its troublesome aspects, and (3) adds new dimensions that conform to modern conceptualizations of reading processes. In designing the IR-TI to accomplish these ends, we made a number of decisions about how the instrument should look, and we conducted careful trials to ensure that it would provide the information we desired. For teachers and other educators interested in the issues involved, this section describes the development process and its rationale.

One Sequence of Graded Word Lists

The IR-TI contains a single graded sequence of word lists, rather than the unnecessary multiple lists included in many commercial instruments. This list consists of words found (1) in each of the two passages at any given level; (2) on the grade-level lists in Dale and O'Rourke's extensive *Living Word Vocabulary* (1976; 1981); and (3) in other large-scale frequency studies (Fry, 1969, 1980; Johnson, 1971; LaPray & Ross, 1969). The word lists also have been extensively field tested with students in grades 1–11. Field investigations have established an average test-retest reliability coefficient of .67 for the lists alone. This result exceeds those reported for many paired cloze tests and most other IRIs.

Initial twenty-item lists were reduced to fifteen words each on the basis of additional field testing. Students at grades 1–11 were first categorized by their classroom or language arts teachers as having average, below-average, or above-average reading ability. After these students were assessed with the word lists, the reduction from twenty to fifteen words was made in order (1) to produce a strong relationship between reading ability and list performance and (2) to produce an overall mean near 75 percent for each list.

The resulting fifteen-word list for each grade level is intended to be presented to students as a whole, rather than word by word in timed and untimed exposures as required by some IRIs.

This policy not only makes the lists easier to administer but also loses no data, since the teacher can still differentiate informally between automatic decoding and the application of analytical skills (Baumann, 1988). The recording form makes this difference clear in each case, in order to make it possible to do later comparisons of automatic proficiency in word recognition with decoding. Such comparisons can be highly informative of a student's individual patterns and processes of decoding (Barr, Sadow, & Blachowicz, 1990).

That some of the words in each list are also found in the passages corresponding to that grade level makes another type of comparison possible. An examiner is able to compare a student's success in pronouncing specific words both in and out of context. Differences attributable to the presence or absence of context can be quite telling (Lipson & Wixson, 1991).

It is also important to note that the place of word lists among diagnostic tools is likely to increase over the next decade, despite the parallel growth in literature-based reading and higher-order literacy. This is because of the steady accumulation of dependable research documenting the limited role of context in reading from the middle grades on and the growing evidence that reliance on context is largely the result of ineffective decoding (Byrne & Fielding-Barnsley, 1991; Foorman, Francis, Novy, & Liberman, 1991; Nicholson, 1991; Rayner & Pollatsek, 1989; Schatz & Baldwin, 1986; Stanovich, 1991; Vellutino, 1991). Hence, access to a carefully designed word-list component is likely to become increasingly important in efficiently estimating reading needs and in guiding students to literature that they can enjoy and from which they can learn.

Two Sequences of Graded Passages

Two parallel sequences of passages permit users to estimate and compare (1) reading and listening ability and (2) silent and oral reading. The IR-TI also provides an extra passage at each grade level, useful in resolving questionable results when they occur. Admittedly, to accomplish all of these goals with no overlap would require four complete passage sequences. Our belief, however, is that instruments this extensive tend to be inefficient, to invite overtesting, to be unnecessarily expensive, and to provide no real advantage over more streamlined instruments. An examiner who devotes one sequence to oral reading, for example, can generally use frustration-level passages in that sequence to estimate listening level while using the second sequence for silent reading and, where needed, for an additional oral passage.

Passages Controlled for Readability

After being composed, the IR-TI passages were subjected to multiple measures of readability. These included the new Fry Short Passage Estimate, the regular Fry formula, the Spache formula (for primary-level passages), and the newer interactive readability measure developed by Zakaluk & Samuels (1988). To avoid the common pitfall of writing passages deliberately to conform to formulas, four steps were taken. First, the initial draft of each passage was composed (or selected) without reference to any formula. Second, where incongruities with formulas were subsequently discovered, revisions were undertaken with care to preserve the coherence of the passage. Third, the interactive formula, which relied on reader judgment, was always administered after revision.

Finally, the resulting sequences of passages were submitted to a panel of library media specialists. Working independently, they rated each passage for naturalness of expression, using a system devised by McKenna and Layton (1990), and judged both of the sequences in their entirety as to whether difficulty did indeed appear to progress in a graduated way. This analysis led to further modifications of language and punctuation.

Passages That Vary in Nature and Encourage Thinking

The passages in the IR-TI are of three types: fictional, nonfictional, and fables or parables. Fables are a specific type of fiction whose purpose will be explained soon. First, however, consider the traditional fictional and nonfictional types of selections chosen.

The passages of the IR-TI are a mix of original and copied material. They were constructed and selected to parallel fictional, nonfictional, and parabolic accounts found either in children's literature or in basal reader programs. Each passage was cross-checked by three readability formulas and field tested by more than forty teachers to be certain it was a fair stand-in for the level of linguistic difficulty of the grade level it was to represent.

Some representations of typical reading were easy to make. For example, the pieces on the desert (grade 3, Form A) and on kites (grade 3, Form B) represent how nonfiction generally is presented to school-age readers, while "The Big Wave" (grade 5, Form A) and "Awaiting the Match" (grade 9, Form B) are representative of fiction. More difficult, but still in our view needing representation, were those once unusual (but no longer so) pieces on the wide variety of topics for which the student is likely to have relatively little explicit prior knowledge and related schemata. This type of "could-be-anything" material is the wonderful surprise of modern-day, literature-based reading programs that deviate from *Reader's Digest* fare and the blandness of earlier basal reading selections. To represent this now-more-common exposure of the uncommon to children, is the passage on art history (grade 1, Form A). This passage about Alexander Calder, the designer of hanging mobiles, was selected because it was the topic of a piece actually found in one widely used literature-based commercial program. We did, however, rewrite the topic to better fit the grade level to which it was addressed, and we also added an illustration so a child could see a concrete representation of a mobile. This, we hoped, would help the child to better relate the account to his or her personal experience. But this is not the major way the IR-TI passages are unique.

The IR-TI passages are considerably different from conventional IRIs through the heavy use of fables. Every other passage is a fable. We had several reasons for using these. The primary reason is that they are parables, which means that each is at least a two-level story: one about what is literally being said and one, at a slightly deeper level, about what it could be taken to mean, or what moral might be derived from it. This two-level structure makes it possible to represent more of the thinking aspects of reading in a relatively short passage. This helps to overcome the criticism that the passages in most IRIs are too brief to represent the type of higher-order thinking one must do in reading longer selections, while it preserves the brevity necessary for evaluation of reading progress with passages at different grade-level equivalents.

One disadvantage of the use of fables in reading assessment is that a student may already be familiar with a given fable and hence is able to answer some questions correctly despite poor reading ability. This shortcoming is largely offset by these further facts:

- Fables are frequently told in slightly different ways and hence are not likely to be identical to the one the pupil may know.

- The fables chosen for the IR-TI are largely unfamiliar to most pupils.

- Comprehension can be further cross-checked by having the student read a like-level passage with different content.

A final point in favor of fables is that their moral undertone is analogous to one of the primary purposes of school, namely to teach pupils to be reflective about themselves and their behavior. To this extent, fables represent a genre that pupils are familiar with, but with content that tends to be interesting, relevant, and challenging.

In brief, fables offer an easier way to answer a basic question about pupil reading: Is the student able to deal with literal and inferential or with more abstract meanings? If you wish to learn more about how to further evaluate abstract and concrete comprehension beyond the IR-TI, see the reference in Appendix A (under "Comprehension") for the ways and means of using proverbs—a sister to fables—in teaching students to improve these higher-order aspects of reading and thinking.

Questions of Two Fundamental Types

Traditional inventories base question types on the literal-inferential hierarchy, though with little attention to critical-constructive responding (e.g., Dale, 1946). Two trends in theory and research indicate that a break with conventional practice is now warranted.

One is the conceptualization of comprehension as an integrative process, during which information across sentences is linked by the reader (e.g., Clark, 1977; Frederickson, 1975; Halliday & Hassan, 1976; Kintsch & van Dijk, 1978; Smith, 1988). Comprehension measures that fail to assess a reader's ability to integrate information across sentence boundaries have been criticized in recent years (Lipson & Wixson, 1991; Shanahan, Kamil, & Tobin, 1982). Consequently, the IR-TI includes questions for each passage that require such integration and that range from straightforward conceptual links to logical, text-based inferences. Inclusion of literal-level questions has not been minimized but has been balanced with better representation of the more transactive and constructivistic aspects of reading and thinking.

This second trend is part of the growing recognition that a reader's personal experiences, culture, and values play a central role in how text is interpreted, sampled, and evaluated. This recognition leads to a vital distinction between attempting to ascertain (reconstruct) an author's meaning, on the one hand, and, on the other, endeavoring to develop (construct) one's personal interpretation of, and response to, what is read (McKenna & Robinson, 1993; Manzo & Manzo, 1993). Importantly, however, these non-text-specific questions have been treated separately so as not to contaminate estimation of text-specific comprehension.

Comprehension questions on the IR-TI are therefore of two major types. *Reconstructive* questions (those that require "reading the lines" and "reading between the lines") assess a student's success in realizing an author's intended message. Such questions recognize the first goal of comprehension, which is "to infer the author's intended meaning" (Johnston, 1983, p. 9). *Constructive* questions (requiring "reading beyond the lines") sample another dimension of the comprehension-thinking process: the reader's ability to conjecture (beyond simple inferences), interpret, connect, and evaluate what has been read. Traditional inventories have either mixed such questions into the comprehension check in an indistinguishable way (hence weakening the reconstructive measure with non-text-specific questions), or they have largely avoided such questions because (1) evaluating students' responses requires some degree of examiner judgment, and (2) the answers are rarely clearly right or wrong, although for purposes of testing we have gravitated on the IR-TI toward the more clearly right and wrong.

Three solutions are offered in the IR-TI to overcome these long-standing problems. First, the IR-TI groups and labels comprehension questions into the two general types mentioned: reconstructive (having answers or their basis in the text) and constructive (requiring critical/creative thinking and use of knowledge beyond the text). Second, it permits users of the IR-TI to afford variable credit based on the reasonableness of the positions reached by a child. Reasonableness is judged in terms of how well the child is able to articulate the process of arriving at a particular interpretation whether or not the test judges it correct or incorrect. And, third, it uses higher-order question types that, frankly, are safe in the sense that few would disagree with what constitutes a "correct" versus an "incorrect" response. (This is much more feasible and less contradictory than it might seem since most mature people are in greater agreement than they realize on most items of judgment. Therefore, estimation of one's ability to think well most often means lining up with the conventional wisdom, rather than against it.)

The delineation of comprehension questions into these two basic types is one of the essential characteristics of the IR-TI, setting it apart from the traditional IRI. This arrangement has the double benefit of: conforming to contemporary views on comprehension and creating an assessment tool that is easy for teachers to conceptualize and use in testing and subsequently in teaching, where impressions gleaned from this inventory can be simultaneously cross-verified and remedied in a variety of reading and discussion situations.

Conventional approaches to question classification, involving numerous comprehension subskills, suffer from a major psychometric difficulty that the IR-TI attempts to avoid. Intersubskill correlations (except for non-text-specific comprehension) generally are so high that the subskill breakdown is useless—the instruments are simply assessing the same global ability (McKenna, 1983; Schell & Hanna, 1981). Although questions in the IR-TI are labeled as to specific skill type (see Figure 2-2), this has been done to acquaint the user with their nature and not to be the *sole* basis of analysis.

Factor analyses involving IR-TI questions have yielded altogether positive results (Manzo & McKenna, 1993). The reconstructive and constructive question types seem to tap distinct factors; however, both clearly are part of the larger process of interactive or "reconstructive and constructive" reading (Manzo & Manzo, 1993; 1994). In other words, the two types correlate but not very highly, so we must rely on good sense to bring them together for comparison—but not to indiscriminately combine them as many inventories do.

Prior Knowledge Assessment

The recognition of the powerful effects of prior knowledge on comprehension (e.g., Pearson, Hansen, & Gordon, 1979; Recht & Leslie, 1988) has led to calls for its assessment before children encounter a passage (e.g., Lipson & Wixson, 1991; Peters & Wixson, 1989). The advantage of estimating the extent of prior knowledge is that erratic results are more likely to be interpretable (McKenna, 1983). For example, a situation in which a student's comprehension is better over a fourth-grade passage than a third-grade one might be explained by superior prior knowledge. A disadvantage of assessing such knowledge is the time required to do so. Holmes and Roser (1987) have suggested five acceptable formats for prior knowledge estimation. The quickest and most straightforward is the use of structured questions. Such questions accompany the IR-TI and have been developed to consume little time in the asking or answering.

Engagement, or Attention and Involvement

The option to *qualitatively* assess the comprehension questions on the IR-TI permits the evaluation of two useful factors: (1) degree of detail or elaboration and (2) congruency/ incongruency. In the first case, the examiner notes the student's tendency to think elaboratively—to the extent that this can be inferred from a student adding relevant details and connections to questions posed. A strong correspondence should occur between this post-reading measure and prior knowledge as estimated before reading. Where it does not, the teacher should prompt elaboration on the post-reading questions to see if the student is shy or thinks it is not appropriate to comment on his or her thoughts and connections during a testing situation. Should the prompts also fail to elicit further details and connections, this result could be taken as an indication of a tendency to read superficially and hence not to *process* and profit by what is read.

The related congruency/incongruency ratio is based largely on simply noting the nature of incorrect responses: Do responses reflect an understanding of the questions (one possibility), or are they so incongruent or mismatched to the questions as to suggest that the student is hardly engaged in the task at hand (for example, *Question*: "What time of day is it in the story? *Answer*: "Wednesday.")? This also is a potentially useful measure of progress for learning disabled (LD), limited English proficiency (LEP), and remedial-level students that may not yet be reflected in markedly improved reading comprehension. The reason for the latter is that a shift in the ratio of incongruent to congruent answers would indicate greater attention to the task and attentive involvement in the interaction with the teacher/examiner. A change following a period of instruction of, say, six weeks (a typical summer program) might show that a student responds to the teacher's questions with a 79 percent congruency ratio (or 21 percent *in*congruency), versus the more typical 50–55 percent congruency ratio (or 45–50 percent incongruency), as was found among students in one such study of one-on-one tutoring provided to severely remedial readers (Manzo, 1969). In general, the congruency ratio tells if students even understand the questions they are being asked, regardless of whether or not they can answer them correctly. We have found this measure to be most strongly related to listening comprehension; thus, a test-retest gain on the congruency ratio tends to mean that the student is listening more attentively during tutoring and other instructional sessions.

Scoring Guides

Each passage is followed by a convenient scoring guide, located just after the "Reading Between the Lines" questions. The guide is useful in quickly categorizing word recognition and compre-hension errors into familiar reading-level designations (independent, instructional, and frustra-tion). The issue of which scoring criteria to use is complex. Some authorities, such as Baumann

(1988); Johnson, Kress, & Pikulski (1987); and McKenna (1983), favor continued use of the criteria proposed by Betts (1946). Others recommend criteria that differ with age (e.g., Lipson & Wixson, 1991; Powell, 1970, 1971; Powell & Dunkeld, 1971). We find Baumann's approach to this issue particularly compelling. He argues that the stricter Betts guidelines sometimes lead to the placement of children in slightly less challenging materials than do more lenient scoring systems. The success they then experience is highly related to their subsequent achievement (Baumann, 1988). In the IR-TI, we have therefore adopted the Betts criteria, and these have served well during field testing. The IRI portion of the IR-TI correlates well, for example, with Silvaroli's (1990) *Classroom Reading Inventory* (Ratanakarn, 1992), another popular IRI that uses the Betts criteria.

SECTION 4 PREPARING TO USE THE IR-TI

Clarifying Your Purpose

Unlike formal tests, which are given in a uniform way for a well-defined purpose, informal measures can be given in a variety of ways, depending on what the teacher/examiner wishes to accomplish. This makes it important to think about how you will use the results so your administration of the instrument will support your aims. Several purposes are typical among IRI users.

Instructional Placement   The most traditional purpose for giving an IRI is to estimate the child's instructional level so proper reading materials can be used. For a large majority of American teachers, this means placing the child at the proper point in a basal reader series. Indeed, this was a central goal of Emmett Betts' pioneering efforts in creating practical IRIs. The IR-TI certainly can be used for this purpose because of the graded nature of the passages it contains.

However, in an era of literature-based instruction, a growing number of teachers have abandoned the basal series for trade books. How can the IR-TI assist these teachers if placement decisions are no longer an issue? Our belief is that knowledge of a child's instructional reading level is just as necessary in literature-based programs as in basal environments. In well-conceived literature-based programs, children are free to select some of the books they read, with the teacher (1) making certain that many titles are available to choose from and (2) offering guidance in the selection process. Knowing the approximate difficulty level of the trade books and the approximate instructional level of the student is the only way to provide such guidance if the result is to be a successful encounter with literature. In addition, many of the books used in such programs are chosen by the teacher—for example, those presented in a big-book format. Here again, knowledge of the match between readability and reading ability is required.

Planning Instruction   Teachers truly interested in meeting students' needs realize the importance of gathering information about literacy development. An IRI is an organized strategy for quickly compiling an array of useful data. Beyond an estimate of reading levels, it has traditionally provided insights into

- Word-recognition strategies used by the reader in context
- The extent of a child's sight-word vocabulary
- Differences in decoding strategies in and out of context
- An estimation of listening ability (and thus oral language development)

These traditional results of an IRI administration are also products of the IR-TI. As previously noted, however, a wealth of additional information, not available from a conventional IRI, also comes from a full application of the IR-TI. Such information includes:

- The child's ability to monitor comprehension
- The extent to which the child can use other higher-order comprehension processes
- The degree of congruence between questions and responses (beyond judgments of mere correctness)

Our belief is that the IR-TI serves teachers better than conventional IRIs as they plan instruction because of its broader base. By viewing thinking as important to literacy, teachers can gain a more complete portrait of the child's development as a reader, writer, and thinker.

Creating Portfolios   Another purpose for giving the IR-TI is to use the results to ground an ongoing assessment portfolio. Two of the most difficult aspects of portfolio development are the time they require to compile and the relative lack of guidance given to teachers in how to organize, manage, and interpret a portfolio's contents (Gomez, Graue, & Bloch, 1991). Because it is broadly based, the IR-TI offers a means of compiling a variety of useful data in an organized and relatively quick manner. We recommend the following steps in using the IR-TI to ground a portfolio:

1. Administer the IR-TI near the beginning of the school year (or at the time a new student joins the class).

2. Place the results in a separate folder for each student.

3. Study the results of the IR-TI for each child to decide which areas will receive instructional emphasis.

4. Periodically add work samples to the portfolio that reflect the child's progress in these areas. Examples include (1) anecdotal evidence jotted down and dated by you; (2) written work, especially when it reflects an area emphasized during instruction; and (3) photocopies of paragraphs read aloud by the child within instructional settings, coded for miscues and dated.

5. Readminister the IR-TI for each child near the end of the year. We recommend that you use the alternate form, but this is not crucial with so much time between tests.

6. Look for evidence of growth in reading level and in those areas you have chosen to emphasize through the year. Photocopy and complete the graphs provided for this purpose (see Figure 4-1).

7. Hold a conference with the child (and possibly one with the parents), during which you clearly indicate how the child has progressed. Cite specific evidence from the two IR-TI administrations and from the work samples between them.

The type of portfolio we have described begins and ends with the IR-TI, with additional evidence sandwiched between the two administrations. Importantly, the selection of that evidence is guided in large part by the child's performance on the first of the two assessments. Not only can the IR-TI be useful in organizing the collection of evidence of a child's growth in literacy, but we suspect it can do much to organize a teacher's thinking about such growth.

Note that blank portfolio charts have been included and that they may be duplicated and customized for any additional purpose.

Using a Strategy for Assessment

Because teachers' purposes for giving the IR-TI will vary, no fixed method of administering it exists. This is a consequence of the informal nature of all IRIs and should be viewed as a strength. The important thing is to clarify your own purpose and then to use the instrument accordingly. Figure 4-2 presents a flowchart describing how the IR-TI might be used to accomplish a variety of purposes.

FIGURE 4-1 IR-TI Portfolio Charts

Student _____

Reading and Listening Levels

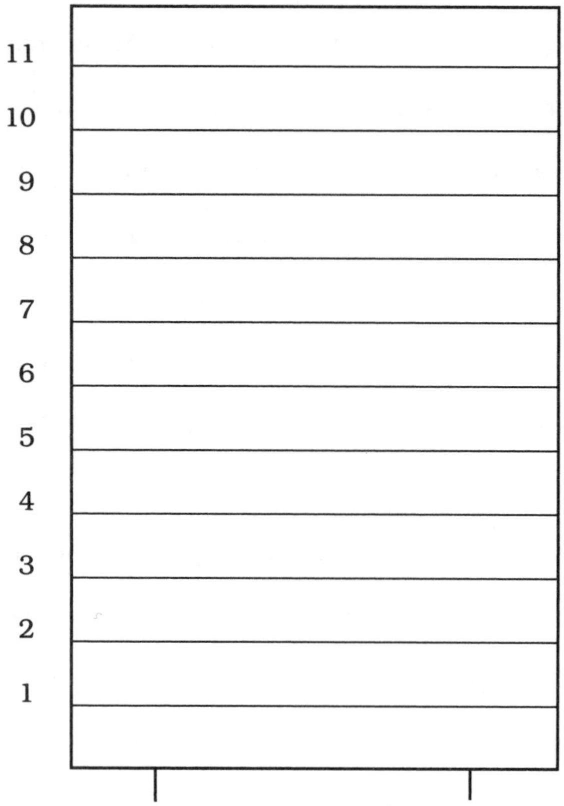

```
11 ┌──────────────────────┐
10 │                      │
 9 │                      │
 8 │                      │
 7 │                      │
 6 │                      │
 5 │                      │
 4 │                      │
 3 │                      │
 2 │                      │
 1 │                      │
   └──────────────────────┘
```

Date 1 _____ Date 2 _____

Instructional _____

Independent _____

Listening _____

Overall Congruency Ratio

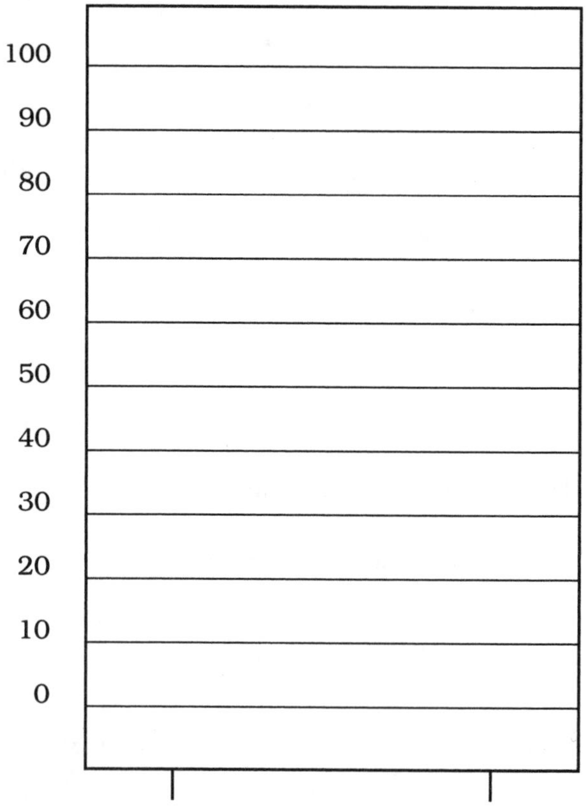

```
100 ┌──────────────────────┐
 90 │                      │
 80 │                      │
 70 │                      │
 60 │                      │
 50 │                      │
 40 │                      │
 30 │                      │
 20 │                      │
 10 │                      │
  0 │                      │
    └──────────────────────┘
```

Date 1 _____ Date 2 _____

Critical/Creative % at Instructional Level

```
100
 90
 80
 70
 60
 50
 40
 30
 20
 10
  0
```

Reading Rate at Instructional Level

```
300
275
250
225
200
175
150
125
100
 75
 50
 25
  0
```

Date 1 _____ Date 2 _____

Date 1 _____ Date 2 _____

Oral Reading   _____

Silent Rereading   _____

Student _____   **Factor Charted** _____

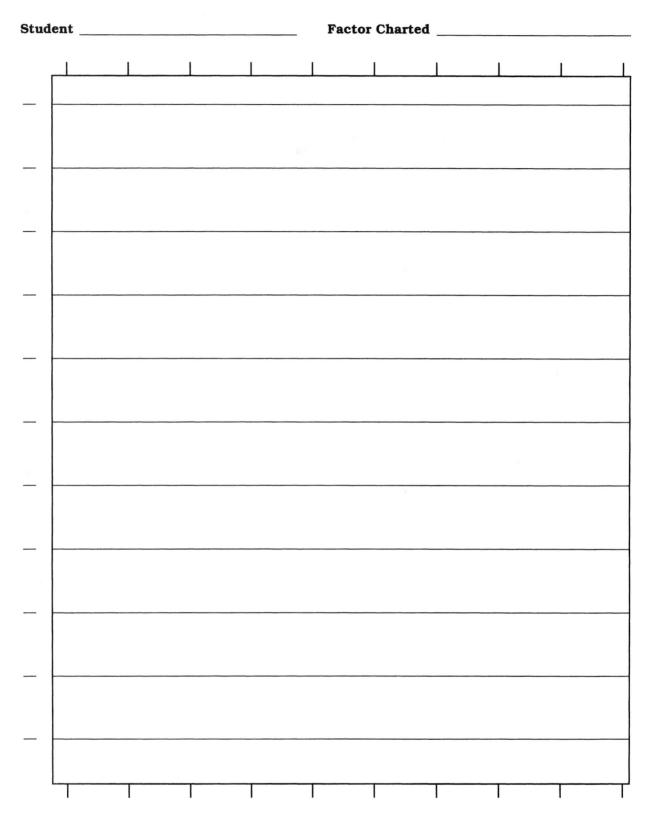

Notes:

FIGURE 4-2 Strategies for Administering the IR-TI

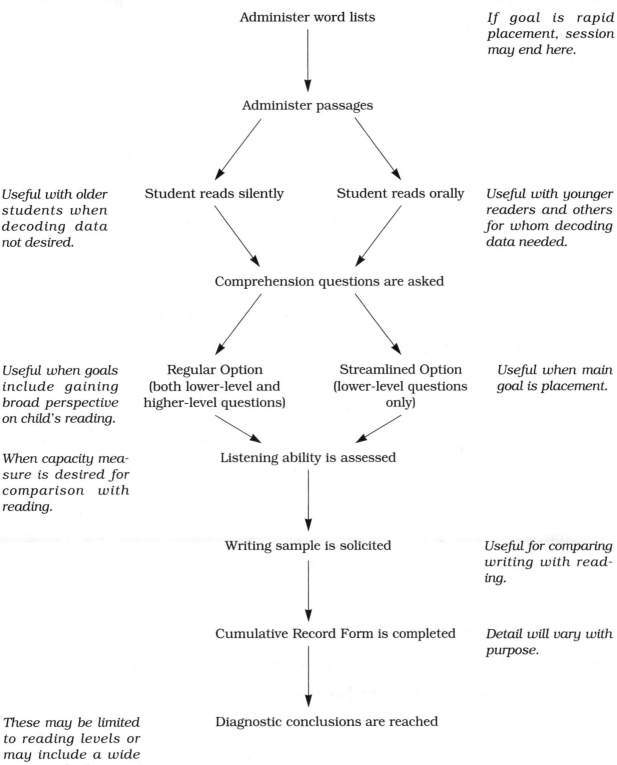

Administer word lists

If goal is rapid placement, session may end here.

Administer passages

Useful with older students when decoding data not desired.

Student reads silently

Student reads orally

Useful with younger readers and others for whom decoding data needed.

Comprehension questions are asked

Useful when goals include gaining broad perspective on child's reading.

Regular Option (both lower-level and higher-level questions)

Streamlined Option (lower-level questions only)

Useful when main goal is placement.

When capacity measure is desired for comparison with reading.

Listening ability is assessed

Writing sample is solicited

Useful for comparing writing with reading.

Cumulative Record Form is completed

Detail will vary with purpose.

These may be limited to reading levels or may include a wide variety of other conclusions.

Diagnostic conclusions are reached

Preparing for the Assessment Session

Once you have clarified your purpose and decided on an assessment strategy that will help you achieve it, you must ensure that the session will go as smoothly as possible. Three issues in particular should be considered: (1) the timing of the session, (2) the place where it will occur, and (3) the materials you will need.

Time   Having clarified your purpose will help you decide how much time the assessment session will require. Other factors make this a matter of guesswork, however. Because students vary considerably in their performance times, because teachers vary in the speed of their administration, and because unforeseen elements (such as the unanticipated need to give an additional passage) may influence the time needed, it is impossible to prescribe guidelines for the amount of time the IR-TI will require. Our experience suggests that sessions tend to vary from ten to thirty minutes. Remember that a session can be discontinued and completed later if your estimate of the time you will need proves too small.

Place   You will need an area free of distractions. A corner of the classroom may suffice, especially when the other children are missing or engaged in work at their desks. A separate, quiet room away from the classroom (e.g., an empty office, a speech carrel, a conference room) may work well, though some authorities suggest that these places can elicit behaviors unlike those the child is likely to exhibit in the classroom setting.

Materials   No matter what your assessment purpose is or what strategy you use in giving the IR-TI, you will need to duplicate parts of the instrument before the session begins. This is because all components of the IR-TI require the teacher/examiner to record student responses in writing, to be compiled and analyzed later. This is the normal use of the test instrument and permission is granted to duplicate the Cumulative Record Form and all Teacher Recording Forms. It is up to the teacher to duplicate in advance of the session whatever materials are likely to be needed.

Three strategies are typically employed to ensure that the materials you need will be available. First, you can estimate which passages and word lists the student is likely to be given and photocopy only these (along with the Cumulative Record Form). Prior experience with the child may provide a fair estimate. This strategy saves paper but runs the risk of not having materials ready when the estimate proves inaccurate. The second strategy is to duplicate the Cumulative Record Form, student copies of all the word lists, and an entire sequence of graded passages. This set can be stapled together and used for all IR-TI options. Its drawback is that paper is inevitably wasted, along with some of the cost of photocopying. The third strategy is to duplicate multiple copies of the various components of the IR-TI and keep them in separate folders to be used as needed during the testing session. One folder would contain the Cumulative Record Form and the rest would contain each of the word cards and passages. In this way, you can pull together the materials actually needed *as they are used*. This is the strategy we recommend, for it conserves cost without sacrificing flexibility.

SECTION 5 ADMINISTERING THE WORD LISTS

The student's performance on the Graded Word Lists provides an estimate of his or her word recognition abilities, with indications of specific areas of strength and weakness in word recognition. This opening section helps the test administrator to determine the level of difficulty at which to begin the Graded Passages portion of the test.

1. Establish a comfortable atmosphere and rapport with the student before proceeding with the inventory.

2. Give the student an idea of why he or she is taking the test. For example, "This test will help me know which books you can read best." Also tell the student that you will write things down so you can remember how well he or she did. You may wish to have the student write his or her name on the Cumulative Record Form. Your name and the date should also be placed on the booklet.

3. Open the Student Test Booklet to the pre-primer level word list, and say, "Pronounce each word for me; if you are not sure or do not know the word, at least tell me what you think it is."

4. Record all responses on the Teacher's Recording Forms, as illustrated. When a list has been completed, ask the student to pronounce each word missed (e.g., "Tell me number 4 again"). Do not follow this procedure if the list is obviously too difficult. See number 5.

    | 1. | and | an / | (error, same error on second trial) |
    | 2. | big | + | (correct, first trial) |
    | 3. | can | dk | (don't know, no correction) |
    | 4. | when | then + | (error on first trial, corrected on second) |
    | 5. | now | 0+ | (word skipped, corrected on second trial) |

5. Discontinue the testing when the student has missed five of the fifteen words on any list. Remember, the reading levels are not determined by this part of the test, so additional testing does not improve the student's score.

6. Total the number of initially correct and self-corrected responses, and record this total at the bottom of each word list administered. Later, record these totals on the Cumulative Record Form, and use the criteria provided at the beginning of the Teacher's Recording Forms to convert them to levels.

7. Since the word lists take very little time to administer, they can be used as a quick screening or quick placement device. Word lists can also be helpful in roughly classifying students as having word recognition ability above, at, or below grade level. (See Figure 5-1 for our recommended criteria for quick placement.)

FIGURE 5-1   Modified Ross-LaPray Word List Criteria*

Independent level	0-1 wrong out of 15
Instructional level	2-4 wrong out of 15
Frustration level	5 or more wrong out of 15

*For convenience, these criteria are reproduced on the Teacher Recording Forms.

SECTION 6 ADMINISTERING THE PASSAGES: REGULAR OPTION

The Form A and B Passages are administered next. This portion of the IR-TI is intended to provide an estimate of the child's independent, instructional, and frustration levels of reading, as well as to identify specific instructional needs related to contextual reading at three levels of comprehension: literal, inferential, and constructive or critical/creative. In this section, the procedures for administering the graded passages are described first in "overview" form and then in complete detail.

Keep in mind that there are many ways to administer the passages, depending on the teacher's purpose for assessment. This section assumes the student will be asked to read the passage orally and that the questions involving "reading beyond the lines," metacognition, interest, and so forth (extensions of the traditional IRI) will be asked. Section 7 presents streamlined procedures, used on traditional IRIs, if these extensions are not desired.

Overview of Administration Procedures

Based on the student's performance on the Graded Word Lists, the teacher/examiner selects the level at which to begin administering the Form A and B Passages. The "Prior Knowledge" questions for the passage are asked first, and the student's responses are briefly recorded. Then the student is shown the passage in the Student Booklet and is asked to read it aloud, while the examiner notes any oral reading deviations from the printed text (as detailed later). The examiner also makes note of the oral reading time. When the student has finished reading, the examiner asks the first question, which, for each passage, is an evaluative question whereby the student is asked to rate his or her enjoyment of or interest in the passage (a scaled "Rating Card" is provided in the Student Booklet). The "Reading the Lines" questions are asked next, and student responses are recorded on the Teacher's Recording Forms. The "Reading Between the Lines" and "Reading Beyond the Lines" questions are asked next, and student responses are recorded. The final question for each passage provides the option of having students make a written response. The detailed procedures listed next include criteria for determining when to discontinue testing.

Detailed Administration Procedures

1. **Decide where to begin testing.**

   For primary-level students, begin at the highest level at which the child scored at the Independent Level (0 or 1 missed) on the word lists.

2. **Introduce the passage, and record student's oral reading performance.**

   - Introduce the oral reading passage by reading the "Prior Knowledge" questions from the Teacher's Recording Form, and briefly record the student's responses.

   - Show the student the passage in the Student Booklet. Ask him or her to read the title and the passage aloud for you, and say that, when he or she has finished, you will ask some questions about the selection.

   - Start a timer (or note the exact time) when the student begins to read.

   - Record any oral reading "miscues" on the passage in the Teacher's Recording Form. Five basic types of word errors are recorded and counted to determine the reading level of the student:

a.	words pronounced by the teacher	P a crowded room
b.	words omitted	a (crowded) room
c.	words inserted	big a crowded room
d.	words substituted	crowned a crowded room
e.	word order reversed	a crowded room

- Guidelines for recording and counting other types of oral reading miscues follow:

word endings   Count the addition or omission of word endings as errors unless the student's oral language reflects the same pattern of addition or omission.

recurring errors   Count the same error only once no matter how many times the error is repeated (for example, when a word is mispronounced early in the passage, and the same mispronunciation is made later in the passage).

hesitations   Hesitations between words and phrases are recorded with slashes— one slash per second (He / saw / the // pirate). If the student pauses for several seconds on coming to an unfamiliar word or asks what a word is, say, "Tell me what you think it is." If the student mispronounces the word, pronounce it aloud yourself (use the prior recording notes *a* and *d*). If a student makes an incorrect pronunciation for a word, and the word is essential to understanding the story, pronounce the word but do not define it (again, using recording notes *a* and *d*).

repetitions   Words or phrases that are repeated should be underlined; neither hesitations nor repetitions are counted as errors, but they should be noted if they are frequent or seem to characterize the way the child reads.

multiple errors   Multiple or consecutive errors are counted as a single error when the second or later errors are brought about in order to maintain grammatical agreement. For example:

$$\frac{\textit{He \quad is}}{\text{They \, are going} \ldots}$$

self-corrections   Errors that are self-corrected by the child are recorded by placing a plus (+) beside the original incorrect substitution and are not counted as errors. For example:

> was +
> He s~~aw~~ a pig. = "He was a pig . . . He saw a pig."

Observations   Additional observations about fluency, word-by-word reading, finger pointing, signs of tension, and so on, should be recorded in the "Notes" section of the Recording Form.

- Record the time when the student completes oral reading.

3. **Ask the "Enjoyment (EJ)" question.**

- Close the Student Booklet, and ask the questions from the Teacher's Recording Forms.

- The first question for each passage is not numbered. It is a self-evaluative question asking the student to rate his or her enjoyment of or interest in the passage. When asking this first question and other rating-scale questions for the passage, hand the student the "Rating Card" to use to indicate his or her response (be sure to explain the response choices the first few times). Use the picture response card for younger children and the nonpicture card for older children.

4. **Ask and score the "Reading the Lines" and "Reading Between the Lines" questions.**

- Read each question in the "Reading the Lines" section, and record all student responses.

- Then ask the "Reading Between the Lines" questions, recording student responses.

- Questions may be rephrased as long as the new wording does not provide additional clues.

- All responses should be recorded. If a student's response is the same as or analogous to the suggested answer (provided in parentheses), the printed answer may simply be underlined, with a different wording written just above or just below the suggested answer. Significantly different responses and incorrect responses should be written in the space provided. In this way, responses can be studied later to check the accuracy of the original scoring or to analyze the reasoning used by the student.

- If the student gives an answer that does not seem to be related to the question, note this (see number 11 on the "congruency ratio"), and repeat the question (e.g., "Listen to the question again . . . "). Write the original response, followed by a "Q" to indicate that the question was repeated, and write the new response.

- Score "1" for a correct response or "0" for an incorrect response. Partial credit may be awarded if the question indicates a specific number, such as, "Name two ways . . . " For such questions, full credit may be given only if at least the specific number of correct responses is given. The question may be repeated if the student names just one, using the recording system described ("Q" to indicate examiner questioning). Many questions provide several suggested answers. Only one answer need be given for total credit, unless the question specifically indicates that a multiple response is required.

- Either during or after testing, you may wish to evaluate the student's responses for "congruency ratio" and for detail. A minus (-) indicates that a given response was not only incorrect but also was incongruent, or irrelevant to the question. In other words, the student's comprehension of the question itself may have been faulty. A plus (+), on the other hand, indicates that an adequately relevant response has been given. Space is provided on the Recording Form to record total scores for congruency and detail. See number 11, "Obtain a congruency ratio," for more specific details.

5. **Ask the first "Metacognition (M)" question.**

6. **Decide when to discontinue silent/oral reading testing.**

   • Testing is discontinued when either the oral reading accuracy reaches frustration level or comprehension falls to approximately 50 percent or less on the questions in the sections labeled "Reading the Lines" and "Reading Between the Lines." Scoring guides on the Teacher's Recording Form indicate which questions to include in this count and how many questions must be correctly answered to continue testing. When the student reaches frustration level in oral reading, the comprehension questions should usually be administered. Inaccurate reading does not always mean that the student will be equally poor in comprehension. If it is evident, after a few questions, that comprehension is also at the frustration level, questioning should be discontinued. When the 50 percent comprehension criterion is reached on the combined questions labeled "Reading the Lines" and "Reading Between the Lines," continue with the "Reading Beyond the Lines" questions for that passage, unless the student is having obvious difficulty, but do not continue to the next passage.

   • The teacher may reasonably test a level above estimated frustration when the first passage score is very low (possible anxiety) or when the score drops rapidly (no apparent reason for suspecting weakness in comprehension).

   • When silent/oral reading testing is discontinued, continue to the next passage for evaluation of listening comprehension (see the number 10 directions).

7. **If comprehension is at least 50 percent on Reading the Lines and Reading Between the Lines, go on to the "Reading Beyond the Lines" questions.**

   • These questions require higher levels of comprehension and thinking. *Before being presented with these "Beyond the Lines" questions, the student should be asked to reread the passage silently.* Say to the student, "Read this passage again, this time silently. When you finish, I will ask you some more questions." Ask the pupil to tell you when he or she finishes and to close the Student Booklet. Proceed, then, with the "Reading Beyond the Lines" questions. Record all responses on the inventory record in the same manner as you did with the Reading the Lines questions.

- Most "Reading Beyond the Lines" questions require qualitative judgments that could be scored on a sliding scale. However, for this first edition we are recommending a simpler correct (1 point), incorrect (0) format.

- Remember, student responses to questions in the "Reading Beyond the Lines" section are not used to determine whether to continue to the next passage: This decision is based on the combined Reading the Lines and Reading Between the Lines questions.

8. **Ask the second Metacognition (M) question.**

9. **Consider the option of collecting a writing sample.**

- The last question for each reading passage is an "Open-Ended" (OE) question. At your discretion, the student may be asked to respond to one of these Open-Ended questions in writing (the Recording Forms include a reminder of this option and space to record evaluative notes). Since the writing sample should be collected for a reading passage at the student's independent or instructional level, this portion of the test should be given on the passage where the student makes his or her first comprehension error. This can be done at the point it occurs or later on, depending on your purpose and the time available.

- Ask the student to respond orally to the question first and then to respond to that same question in writing. There should be evidence that the student is able to represent his or her oral response in writing. Ideally, a student's written rendition should reflect even greater thought or deeper processing as a result of reflecting, talking it through, and then writing. However, most remedial-level readers have less practice in writing than in reading; hence, their oral responses initially may be superior to the written ones. This situation also would point to the need to provide more opportunities for writing.

- The time limit for writing even a brief response should be generous, and the examiner should not appear to be hovering in wait. This can be accomplished by having the student go to another part of the room to write. The interim period is a good time to score the inventory to that point or to begin testing other students.

- Appendix B contains guidance for evaluating writing samples produced.

10. **When oral/silent reading is discontinued, use the next passage to assess listening comprehension.**

- Assessment of listening comprehension is optional but strongly recommended. Such assessment provides a rough estimate of reading "expectancy," the level at which the student should be expected to read and comprehend with further instruction. The listening measure also is known as an assessment of "capacity," since it strongly parallels the findings derived from comprehensive intelligence tests.

- When you have decided to discontinue oral/silent reading, go to the next passage and begin by reading and discussing the "Prior Knowledge" questions. Then tell the student to listen carefully in order to answer questions about the passage. Read the passage to the student while he or she listens. Ask the first two sets of questions (Reading the Lines and Reading Between the Lines), and record the student's responses. If the student's comprehension is 70 percent or higher on the first two sets of questions, go on to the next passage, following the same procedure. (Administer all three sets of questions, but use only the first two sets as the criteria for discontinuing testing.)

- Discontinue the listening assessment when comprehension on the first two sets of questions falls below 70 percent.

11. **Obtain a "Congruency Ratio."**

- The student's response to each question is evaluated in terms of whether it is reasonably related to the question (even if it is incorrect) or it is so far afield as to indicate that the child misunderstood the question or is totally inattentive to the task at hand. This "congruency count" estimates the student's *engagement,* or attention, interest, and attitude toward reading.

- To obtain the congruency count, rescore the student's responses to all comprehension questions—based on reading or listening—as either *congruent* (coded with a plus sign) or *incongruent* (coded with a minus sign). Count the number answered congruently and what percentage this represents of the total number of questions asked (e.g., 5 congruent divided by 10 asked = 50 percent congruency).

- This measure is more sensitive than the comprehension score and hence can be used as a quantitative indicator of possible progress in commitment to learning or, conversely, as further evidence of lack of sufficient engagement to read, comprehend, and think effectively.

- This measure can be especially useful in detecting intimations of progress for children from different language backgrounds, children with learning disabilities, children with diminished mental capacity, and children with poor orientation toward reading, since progress for all four of these groups of readers, even though they are otherwise quite different, is likely to be slower.

12. Obtain the "Reconstructive/Constructive (R/C) Ratio."

- To establish a rough estimate of the ratio of "Reconstructive" (literal and inferential) comprehension to "Constructive" (evaluative, applied, critical/creative) comprehension, merely count the number of answers correct out of the number tried on each passage. Then compare percentages. For example, if a child answered 6 of 8 reconstructive questions and 2 of 6 constructive questions, the "R/C" ratio would be 75:33.

SECTION 7 ADMINISTERING THE PASSAGES: STREAMLINED OPTION

As we have stated, the IR-TI is constructed "around" a traditional IRI and can be used as such. It may be helpful to think of the IR-TI as "containing" an IRI. A teacher/examiner whose purposes on a given occasion are somewhat modest (instructional placement, for example) may desire the more conventional—and certainly far quicker—option of using only the traditional IRI that lies within.

Most of the differences between the regular and streamlined options involve comprehension assessment. The streamlined option entails asking fewer questions and making fewer judgments. Rather than provide detailed directions, we have compiled a step-by-step chart (Figure 7-1) for quick reference in comparing the two options and in remembering the sequence to follow in either option. As you gain experience with the IR-TI, use the chart as a quick reference whenever needed. Refer to Section 6 for details.

FIGURE 7-1   Passage Administration Quick Reference

Regular Option	Streamlined Option
Decide which passage to use first.	Decide which passage to use first.
Introduce the passage.	Introduce the passage.
Ask Prior Knowledge questions (PK).	Ask Prior Knowledge questions (PK).
Start timer.	
Record miscues as student reads aloud.	Record miscues as student reads aloud.
Record reading time when student finishes.	
Ask Evaluation (EV) question.	
Ask Reading the Lines questions.	Ask Reading the Lines questions.
Ask Reading Between the Lines questions.	Ask Reading Between the Lines questions.
Ask first Metacognition (M) question.	
Determine if comprehension is at least 50 percent.	Determine if comprehension is at least 50 percent.
If not, consider next passage for listening.	If not, consider next passage for listening.
If so, ask student to reread passage silently.	If so, decide on next passage to use.
Make congruency judgments (or do so later).	
Ask Reading Beyond the Lines questions.	
Ask second Metacognition (M) question.	
Ask Open-Ended (OE) question.	
Consider writing sample based on OE.	
Decide on next passage to use.	

SECTION 8 COMPLETING THE CUMULATIVE RECORD FORM

Begin by transcribing information from the individual passages of the Teacher Recording Forms onto the Cumulative Record Form. Having this information available in a single chart makes interpreting it quite manageable. A blank Cumulative Record Form (Figure 8-1) appears on page 51, and it should be copied as needed.

Note that the Cumulative Record Form is designed to accommodate virtually any use of the IR-TI. Space is provided for the results of the word lists, of the silent and oral passages, and of the listening passages. Also, appropriate rows are given for recording the information resulting from the Regular Option for administering the passages. Chances are, there is more room on the Cumulative Record Form than you will need. If, for example, the Streamlined Option is chosen, or if listening is not assessed, or if administration of the IR-TI is abbreviated in some other way, not all of the form will be used.

Example

Figure 8-2 presents a completed example of the Cumulative Record Form. Word lists PP through grade 4 have been given, and the examiner has used the criteria from Figure 5-1 to convert the number missed on each list into a level. The highest independent-level list (grade 2) was used to identify the level of the first passage given.

While the example does not include the actual coded oral passage, we can see that the examiner has tallied the number of miscues and looked up the corresponding level in the "Scoring Guide" at the end of the Recording Form for the Form A / Grade 2 passage ("The Crab and His Mother"). This level (independent) has been abbreviated by the examiner in the space provided on the "Word Recognition Level" line. The student then answered all three of the "Prior Knowledge" questions satisfactorily, and 100 percent has been entered in the space. On the "rabbit" scale of 1 to 5, the student rated the level of enjoyment as 4. The examiner has then totaled the number of correct answers to the Reading the Lines and Reading Between the Lines sections, has entered the percentage correct, and has looked up the appropriate performance level (IND) for that total in the Scoring Guide.

The "Overall Passage Level" was determined by comparing the student's "Word Recognition Level" and "Comprehension Level" for the grade 2 passage. (The method of determining the Overall Passage Level is to use the lower of the Word Recognition and Comprehension levels. This approach will be further explained in Section 10.) Next, the Reading Beyond the Lines percentage has been recorded. Relatively few questions of this kind occur for each passage, so the examiner can easily figure the percentage. The next two lines are for the Metacognition questions. (Recall that the first is located after the Reading Between the Lines section and the second after the Reading Beyond the Lines section.) Again, the numbers recorded are the "rabbit" ratings (1 to 5). The next line is for the Congruency Ratio. This the number of congruent answers to the Reading the Lines and Reading Between the Lines questions, followed by a slash and the total number of such questions asked. For the grade 2 passage, there were 7 questions at this level, of which the student's answers were judged to be congruent for 6 of them. The last line is for the Reconstructive/Constructive Ratio. The examiner has recopied the percentage for Reading the Lines and Reading Between the Lines and the percentage for Reading Beyond the Lines as a ratio. Two more passages were administered, and the results were recorded in the same way.

Because the grade 4 passage was judged to be frustrating, the grade 5 passage was then given as a listening passage. For the Reading the Lines and Reading Between the Lines questions, the percent correct was 89. For the Reading Beyond the Lines questions, the percentage was 50. The overall levels have been recorded at the bottom of the form, after having been arrived at through a method described in Section 10. Finally, the Overall Congruency Ratio has been computed by the examiner by first adding all the congruent responses (on both reading and listening passages) and then dividing by the number of questions judged. In this case, 23 of 31 answers were thought to be congruent, and the percentage (74 percent) has been recorded.

Example **51**

FIGURE 8-1   IR-TI Cumulative Record Form

Student _____   Examiner _____   Date of Test _____

Grade _____   Sex _____   Age _____   School _____   Date of Birth _____

Word Lists

Level	PP	P	1	2	3	4	5	6	7	8	9	10	11
Result													

Passages

Form									
Level									
Word Recognition Level									
Prior Knowledge %									
Enjoyment (EJ)									
Comprehension % (Lines + Between)									
Comprehension Level (Lines + Between)									
Overall Passage Level									
Beyond Lines %									
Metacognition (1st question)									
Metacognition (2nd question)									
Congruency Ratio									
Reconstructive/Constructive Ratio									

Listening

Level	1	2	3	4	5	6	7	8	9
Form									
% (Lines + Between)									
% (Beyond)									

Estimated Levels: **Examiner Notations**

Independent   _____

Instructional   _____

Frustration   _____

Listening   _____

Overall Congruency Ratio   _____

FIGURE 8-2   IR-TI Cumulative Record Form Example

Student _____   Examiner _____   Date of Test _____

Grade _____   Sex _____   Age _____   School _____   Date of Birth _____

Word Lists

Level	PP	P	1	2	3	4	5	6	7	8	9	10	11
Result	IND	IND	IND	IND	INS	FRU							

Passages

Form	A	A	A					
Level	2	3	4					
Word Recognition Level	IND	INS	FRU					
Prior Knowledge %	100	67	100					
Enjoyment (EJ)	4	3	4					
Comprehension % (Lines + Between)	100	75	71					
Comprehension Level (Lines + Between)	IND	INS	INS					
Overall Passage Level	IND	INS	FRU					
Beyond Lines %	50	80	67					
Metacognition (1st question)	4	3	1					
Metacognition (2nd question)	3	3	3					
Congruency Ratio	6/7	6/8	3/7					
Reconstructive/Constructive Ratio	100:50	75:80	71:67					

Listening

Level	1	2	3	4	5	6	7	8	9
Form					A				
% (Lines + Between)					89				
% (Beyond)					50				

Estimated Levels: **Examiner Notations**

Independent   2

Instructional   3

Frustration   4

Listening   5

Overall Congruency Ratio   74

SECTION 9 DETERMINING READING AND LISTENING LEVELS

Determining reading and listening levels is usually straightforward, although irregular results can sometimes prevent adequate estimates. This section offers standard guidelines for estimating these levels.

Reading Levels

Estimating a child's independent, instructional, and frustration level is a two-part process. First, the child's performance on each passage read must be classified. Second, the resulting passage judgments are considered together to determine the overall reading levels.

Classifying Performance on a Passage When the child has finished answering the Reading the Lines and Reading Between the Lines questions, the teacher/examiner can evaluate performance on that passage by following these steps.

1. Determine the number of correct responses to these questions (considering only questions in the Reading the Lines and Reading Between the Lines sections).

2. Find the total in the ranges given in the Scoring Guide at the end of the questions. (Record the percentage correct if you wish, though you will not need it to classify the passage.)

3. Abbreviate the resulting level on the Cumulative Record Form.

4. If the passage has been read silently, this result is also the Overall Passage Level, and it should be written again on that line.

5. If the passage has been read orally, determine the number of countable errors, using the guidelines given in Section 6.

6. Find this total in the ranges given in the Scoring Guide at the end of the questions.

7. Write the result on the Cumulative Record Form.

8. For passages read orally, the Word Recognition Level and the Comprehension Level must be considered together to determine the Overall Passage Level. When these two

Levels are the same, they are naturally the same as the Overall Level. When they differ, a good rule of thumb is that *the Overall Passage Level is the lower of the two.*

Determining the Reading Levels   Once the Overall Passage Level has been determined for each of the passages read by the student, you are ready to estimate the independent, instructional, and frustration levels. Ideally, the independent level will be lower than the instructional, which will be lower than the frustration level. In fact, if this situation does not occur, the assessment has gone awry. (Prior Knowledge and Enjoyment questions may help to tell why.) At this point we will restate the definitions, provided in Section 2, of the three levels:

Independent Level =   Highest level at which comprehension is good *without help*

Instructional Level =   Highest level at which comprehension is good *with help*

Frustration Level   =   Lowest level at which comprehension is poor *even with help*

We now offer several brief examples of various sets of results and of how an examiner might interpret them. Keep in mind, however, that it is impossible to outline in advance every set of circumstances that may arise.

Example One   A student has read aloud the grades 2, 3, and 4 passages of Form A. The examiner has used the Scoring Guide for each passage to convert the number of oral reading errors and the number of comprehension errors into levels.

Level	2	3	4					
Word Recognition Level	IND	INS	FRU					
Prior Knowledge %								
Enjoyment (EJ)								
Comprehension % (Lines + Between)								
Comprehension Level (Lines + Between)	IND	INS	FRU					
Overall Passage Level								

The next step is to arrive at an overall judgment for each passage. Since no conflicts occurred between word recognition and comprehension performance, it is easy to reach an overall judgment about the student's performance at each of the three levels assessed. These labels should be written in as follows:

Level	2	3	4					
Word Recognition Level	IND	INS	FRU					
Prior Knowledge %								
Enjoyment (EJ)								
Comprehension % (Lines + Between)								
Comprehension Level (Lines + Between)	IND	INS	FRU					
Overall Passage Level	IND	INS	FRU					

Finally, you must arrive at an estimate of the student's independent, instructional, and frustration levels. In a clearcut case like this one, the conclusion is obvious. The levels are then noted at the bottom of the Cumulative Record Form:

Estimated Levels:

Independent	2
Instructional	3
Frustration	4

Example Two Unfortunately, reading assessment cannot always be done so precisely. Let us consider a less clearcut example. This time, some of the scores have fallen into the borderline region between the instructional and frustration levels. We will abbreviate this region as "I/F."

Level	2	3	4					
Word Recognition Level	IND	I/F	FRU					
Prior Knowledge %								
Enjoyment (EJ)								
Comprehension % (Lines + Between)								
Comprehension Level (Lines + Between)	IND	I/F	FRU					
Overall Passage Level	IND	I/F	FRU					

In this case, no definite instructional level can be identified. The examiner must make a judgment based on the results. A useful strategy is to consider performance across passages. A quick glance reveals that the student's outcomes have steadily declined, reaching frustration at grade 4. Grade 3 seems the best estimate of the instructional level, even though that passage appeared to be slightly harder than one might expect at the instructional level.

Example Three   What happens when the student's performance is stretched out across a number of readability levels? A student may have performed comparably at adjacent levels, despite the difficulty factor. In such cases, an accepted rule of thumb is to look for the highest level at which performance was independent or instructional and the lowest at which performance was frustration. (Recall the definitions stated earlier.) As always, of course, there is plenty of room for professional judgment, and any examiner should feel free to overrule such a guideline if circumstances appear to warrant it. The following results illustrate a fairly typical situation in which the rule of thumb we have just stated can be used:

Level	2	3	4	5	6			
Word Recognition Level	IND	IND	INS	INS	FRU			
Prior Knowledge %								
Enjoyment (EJ)								
Comprehension % (Lines + Between)								
Comprehension Level (Lines + Between)	IND	IND	INS	INS	FRU			
Overall Passage Level	IND	IND	INS	INS	FRU			

On the basis of these results, the higher of the two independent levels and the higher of the two instructional levels would be recorded:

Estimated Levels:

Independent	3
Instructional	5
Frustration	6

Example Four So far we have examined only cases in which the word recognition and comprehension levels are consistent. When the two differ, we rely on the rule of thumb stated previously: *Use the lower (worse) of the two levels as the Overall Passage Level.* This example, which appears a bit confusing at first, has a result identical to "Example One."

Level	2	3	4					
Word Recognition Level	IND	IND	INS					
Prior Knowledge %								
Enjoyment (EJ)								
Comprehension % (Lines + Between)								
Comprehension Level (Lines + Between)	IND	INS	FRU					
Overall Passage Level	IND	INS	FRU					

Estimated Levels:

Independent	2
Instructional	3
Frustration	4

Example Five Now let us look at the erratic case in which a student performs better on a higher-level passage than on a lower one. In this situation, the Prior Knowledge questions can often help resolve such a seemingly inexplicable outcome.

Level	3	4						
Word Recognition Level	INS	IND						
Prior Knowledge %	33	100						
Enjoyment (EJ)								
Comprehension % (Lines + Between)								
Comprehension Level (Lines + Between)	INS	IND						
Overall Passage Level								

How can a student's instructional level be lower than the independent level? In reality, it cannot. Measurement problems can sometimes give that impression, however. Note that the student's prior knowledge of the grade 4 passage was substantially stronger than for the grade 3 passage. In a case like this, greater credence should be given the grade 4 performance, since it reflects what the student can do when prior knowledge is adequate. Since knowledge-building activities accompany nearly any instructional technique (e.g., the Directed Reading Activity, Directed Reading–Thinking Activity, etc.), this policy seems justified.

Another useful indicator in dealing with anomalous results is the student's response to the Enjoyment (EJ) question. Recall that this question is asked just after the student reads. It attempts to determine interest level, which is correlated with, but is not the same as, prior knowledge. Had the student in this example exhibited adequate prior knowledge for both passages, the Enjoyment question might have revealed a greater interest in the harder passage.

Example Six   Occasionally, inconsistencies and borderline results can create a situation in which a reasonable interpretation is difficult. If you are convinced the student is trying and if you judge decoding skills to be beyond the primer (early first grade) level, consider administering a passage from Form B. Let us return to Example Five, assuming this time that prior knowledge of the two passages was adequate and that motivation, as indicated by the evaluation question, was strong in both cases. The examiner may elect to give an alternative passage at either of the two levels already assessed:

	A	A	B					
Form								
Level	3	4	4					
Word Recognition Level	INS	IND	IND					
Prior Knowledge %	100	100	100					
Enjoyment (EJ)								
Comprehension % (Lines + Between)								
Comprehension Level (Lines + Between)	INS	IND	1ND					
Overall Passage Level								

Here, the additional passage helps to resolve the inconsistency. This student's poorer performance at the grade 3 level, while still not explained, no longer requires explanation. The student has exhibited the same strong performance on a second grade 4 passage. The use of alternative passages can often resolve results that are hard to interpret. Even when such passages are given, however, all doubts may not disappear.

Example Seven Beginning readers (and readers experiencing problems) may lack a true independent level. The following results are typical and do not suggest that additional testing is needed to try to establish an independent level, for it probably does not yet exist.

	1	2						
Level								
Word Recognition Level	INS	FRU						
Prior Knowledge %								
Enjoyment (EJ)								
Comprehension % (Lines + Between)								
Comprehension Level (Lines + Between)	INS	FRU						
Overall Passage Level	INS	FRU						

Listening Level

In Section 2, we defined the Listening Level as the highest level for which there is good comprehension when the passage is read aloud to the student by the teacher. Numerically speaking, we look for the highest level at which the comprehension percentage (Reading the Lines plus Reading Between the Lines) is 70 percent or more. A rather dependable way of estimating where to begin in the search for the Listening Level is to choose the passage directly above the estimated Frustration Level, once it has been established. If this produces a comprehension percentage considerably more than 70, the next-higher passage may be administered. Consider the following results:

Level	1	2	3	4	5	6	7	8	9
Form					A	A	A		
% (Lines + Between)					89	78	57		

Here, the initial passage yielded a high percentage score, and the examiner chose to proceed to the next-higher passage (grade 6). Whether it was wise to continue to grade 7 after a percentage score of 78 resulted at grade 6 is debatable. In any event, the Listening Level suggested by these results is grade 6.

SECTION 10 REACHING ADDITIONAL DIAGNOSTIC CONCLUSIONS

Determining a child's reading levels will always be an important part of an IRI interpretation. Often, however, the test administration offers far deeper insights into a child's development as a reader. This is especially so, we believe, of the IR-TI, since it has been designed specifically to extend and vary the array of data available to the teacher. In this section, we offer suggestions for using these data to arrive at additional conclusions.

Identifying Reader Characteristics

One of the more subjective—and potentially one of the most rewarding—aspects of interpreting the results of an IR-TI administration is the search for revealing trends in the data. Like other IRIs, the IR-TI makes possible an analysis of oral reading errors (miscues). Unlike other instruments, it permits a reasonable comparison of comprehension levels (literal versus inferential versus critical), and it affords a reliable look at a student's metacognition. We do not wish to limit the interpretive thinking of teachers using the IR-TI, but we believe a few guidelines can be helpful at the outset.

Patterns of Comprehension   Once you have determined the instructional level, confine your analyses to passages at that level or below. Frustration-level passages probably are not characteristic of comprehension patterns exhibited by the student when decoding and comprehension are both adequate. (Exceptions to this policy involve the Metacognitive questions and the value ratings. We will discuss these later.)

For passages at and below the instructional level, you can use the charts to determine the percentage of correct answers on the Reading the Lines and Reading Between the Lines questions. A separate chart helps determine the percentage of acceptable answers to the Reading Beyond the Lines questions. Spaces are given on the Cumulative Record Form to record these two percentages for each passage. You may recall from Section 9 that these are the two percentages used for the Reconstructive/Constructive Ratio. To illustrate, let us return to an extended version of Example Three (Section 9) and assume that the Reading Beyond the Lines questions have been asked for each passage (after permitting the student to reread each passage silently). In that example, five passages were administered, but the last was judged at the frustration level, so it will be excluded from our comprehension pattern analysis. (Note that Reading Beyond the Lines questions were not asked by the examiner at the sixth level after frustration level was reached on the easier questions.)

Level	2	3	4	5	6			
Word Recognition Level	IND	IND	INS	INS	FRU			
Prior Knowledge %	100	100	100	100	100			
Enjoyment (EJ)	5	4	4	4	2			
Comprehension % (Lines + Between)	100	100	75	80	50			
Comprehension Level (Lines + Between)	IND	IND	INS	INS	FRU			
Overall Passage Level	IND	IND	INS	INS	FRU			
Beyond Lines %	100	83	100	50				
Metacognition (1st question)	5	5	4	5	2			
Metacognition (2nd question)	5	4	5	3				
Congruency Ratio	100	100	86	80	56			
Reconstructive/Constructive Ratio	100:100	100:83	75:80	80:50				

You may have wondered why we have not made it convenient to compute separate percentages for literal (Reading the Lines) and inferential (Reading Between the Lines) questions. This is because the correlation between such scores typically is so great that there is little advantage to be gained by looking at these two types of questions independently (Schell & Hanna, 1981). Our approach has been to combine them as two aspects of the same factor—*reconstructive* comprehension—and then to compare the result with the student's performance on the critical/creative (Reading Beyond the Lines) questions, which reflect *constructive* comprehension. The correlation between reconstructive and constructive comprehension performance is not nearly so predictable, and the contrast is likely to have useful instructional implications (Manzo & McKenna,

1993). Our means of making that contrast is the Reconstructive/Constructive Ratio. As you can see from the example, this is created simply by rewriting the two percentages in ratio form. For this student, it appears no pattern arises in which one of the two percentages is typically lower than the other. Note how the easier passages have allowed the student to exhibit good responses to the higher-order questions—a positive result. It is a good idea to look for a critical/creative score that may be markedly below the literal/inferential score. Such a pattern is typical of remedial students, but, again, it is not characteristic of this one.

Curiously, where overall reading has been weak, an instructional program stressing critical and creative reading and thinking activities has been shown to be a sound means of improving *basic* reading (Collins, 1992; Haggard, 1977; Manzo & Manzo, 1993).

Higher-Order Thinking Occasionally (we estimate about 15 percent of the time), remedial-level students will handle Reading Beyond the Lines questions very well. This should be taken as a good sign. It generally means that the student is attempting to compensate for limited reading ability by making as many thoughtful connections as possible in order to make sense and meaning. This apparent oddity is supported by Stanovich's (1980) interactive-compensatory model of reading. It basically suggests that a student brings the context of his or her life experiences fully to bear on a passage whose meanings and context cannot be ascertained by conventional reading. Since the student is working with few word and passage cues and a disproportionate number of external connections, you also can expect an erratic pattern on these conjectural questions, which would sometimes appear remarkably insightful and full and other times completely off the mark.

More frequently (about 20 percent of the time), relatively proficient readers—those reading at or above grade-level expectation on the literal and inferential questions—do quite poorly on the Reading Beyond the Lines, or critical and constructive, questions. This is a more serious condition, in our judgment, than typically is acknowledged and one that the IR-TI is uniquely designed to discern. A pattern of weak constructive/critical responses to text is an indication that the student is essentially a passive reader and one who will need encouragement in connecting reading to other school subjects and to life experiences. Such students rarely are able to transfer learning and to form sound concepts or to solve problems unless guided in doing so. The recommended means of drawing such students into higher-order thinking is to ask them more questions that require conjectural and evaluative thinking. Questions such as, "What do you think or feel about this?" and "What do you suppose happened before, or following this event?" tend to strengthen connections to other stories, school learnings, and human experiences.

Metacognition   At two times for each passage, the student is asked to rate his or her own comprehension, once for the literal and inferential questions and again for the critical/creative questions. These two checkpoints provide indicators of the extent to which the student is aware of comprehension difficulties. Recall that the student's response is a rating from 1 to 5, with 5 the most positive. The diagnostic value of these ratings lies in comparing them with actual comprehension performance. In our example, the relationship between the student's self-rating and the actual comprehension scores is strong. Both in the case of lower-level and of higher-order comprehension, this student seems highly aware of how well she or he has understood. Note that we now find even the frustration-level passage useful for comparison with the student's self-appraisal: A poor performance (FRU) is mirrored by a low self-appraisal (2).

Value Ratings   Recording the number of responses that (1) tend to be well articulated or elaborated or (2) tend to lack congruence with the gist of the passage can provide additional insights into comprehension patterns. In general, as the passages increase in difficulty, the number of detailed responses can be expected to decrease and the number of incongruent answers to increase. This is not always the case, however. Students who are good comprehension monitors tend to realize when their understanding has grown weak, and they may simply decline to answer. Incongruent answers are one indicator of a student's metacognitive ability. Another is, of course, the metacognitive questions themselves ("How well do you think you answered . . . "), and these two indicators should be compared against actual comprehension. It is hoped that poor comprehension will be associated with (1) the realization that a problem exists (low self-ratings on the metacognitive questions) and (2) the absence of a tendency to produce aberrant, or untrue-to-type, responses. In the example, a steady decline is evident in the percentage of Reading the Lines and Reading Between the Lines answers that the examiner has judged to be congruent. (Note that since congruency is based on these two levels and not on the Reading Beyond the Lines questions, the Congruency Ratio can be computed even for a passage at the frustration level.)

Another useful perspective on value ratings is to compare them with prior knowledge levels and to word recognition performance. For example, a passage that the student has read with good oral accuracy and for which strong prior knowledge has been demonstrated should not lead to incongruent responses. A tendency to produce them under these favorable circumstances may reveal a significant reading comprehension problem. Where prior knowledge is weak or where decoding is error prone, the student may lack the tools to produce even congruent answers. In these cases, however, the examiner should be more concerned about the tendency not to monitor comprehension (i.e., not to realize that answers are incongruous). Incongruous responding also can be an indication of lapsed attention and fatigue. A retest on a comparable passage following a rest period can be used to confirm or refute this possibility.

Oral Error Patterns   We concede that miscue analysis is a less-than-perfect way to study the reading strategies used by a given student (see Rayner & Pollatsek, 1989). For this reason, we do not recommend the laborious analytical procedures involved in some test instruments. We suggest that important insights can be gained, however, by informal inspection of oral errors in search of significant trends.

Perhaps the most important consideration is the degree to which errors reflect a reliance on context to identify words. Greater reliance is to be expected on the part of beginning readers and poorer older readers (Nicholson, 1991; Stanovich, 1980). In other words, the natural developmental trend is toward less reliance on context and more on accuracy in word recognition and analysis. To gauge the extent of reliance, an examiner must, as with comprehension performance, limit consideration to passages at or below the instructional level. (As a reader approaches the frustration level, context simply cannot be used.) Especially important are word substitutions, for these can be readily evaluated in terms of their suitability in context. Substituting a word like *pony* for *horse* is a tendency we may well expect to see among beginners but that should give way to attempts to pronounce unfamiliar words as decoding sophistication improves.

In your inspection of coded passages at the instructional level or below, you may find these specific suggestions helpful:

1. Less able readers tend to substitute real words rather than phonic approximations.

2. Omissions tend to be most prevalent among beginning readers, who tend to have limited decoding strategies, and they gradually give way to substitutions.

3. Letter reversals (e.g., *was* for *saw*) tend to be rare and generally disappear by second grade.

4. Insertions are likewise generally rare; their prevalence may signal overreliance on context. They also tend to occur when incompatibility between the child's language and the language patterns of the passage exist.

5. A large number of teacher-supplied pronunciations (coded "P") may reveal a lack of adequate decoding skills or an unwillingness to apply them. They also may be accompanied by good comprehension, since the student is being supplied with correct words.

6. Repetitions and self-corrections generally signal the student's attempt to monitor comprehension and word recognition. They therefore provide an informal indicator of metacognitive activity. They are a welcome sign as materials become more difficult.

7. The total absence of errors (word-perfect reading) generally indicates a strong sight vocabulary but may not always be accompanied by good comprehension. A student

with near-perfect word recognition and limited comprehension is often termed a "word caller."

8. Miscues made in context are often different from attempts to pronounce the same words in isolation. Make a point of comparing the two conditions for words that appear both in the lists and in the passages. These are underlined in the teacher's copy of the passages.

The following additional guidelines were offered by Wixson (1979) in her review of research conducted into miscue analysis:

9. Most miscues are syntactically acceptable, but fewer are semantically acceptable.

10. Beginning readers tend to substitute words they have already seen in print. As they mature, they are more likely to substitute words they have never seen and to substitute nonwords. (Note that this suggests that these seemingly more chaotic responses may have more order and progress than you might first believe. Therefore, be hopeful: Time and further instruction should convert these seemingly erratic responses to correct word identifications.)

11. Less proficient readers tend to make fewer self-corrections than better readers.

12. Proficient readers tend to omit known words that are not essential to understanding.

Word Recognition in and out of Context   Another way to judge a student's reliance on context is to compare attempts to pronounce the same words in and out of context (Lipson & Wixson, 1991; Manzo & Manzo, 1993). The IR-TI makes this comparison simple by arranging for two or more words in each of the Form A passages to be included in the word list at that grade level. These words are underlined in the teacher's copy of the passages for easy reference, followed by subscripts telling the list in which each appears. If several passages have been read aloud by the student, the number of words that can be compared in this way may be sizable. Like miscue analysis, however, we recommend considering only those words appearing in passages that you judge to be at or below the student's instructional level so context is available to be used if desired. For Form A passages at grades 5–9, the only underlined words are those appearing in the word list at that grade level. Other words will always occur in these passages (e.g., *the*, *a*, *of*, etc.) that appear in lower-level lists. These words also might prove useful in making comparisons.

We suggest creating a simple chart to record your comparisons. Simply write how the child responded in and out of context. Then examine the results to determine if a pattern is evident.

Example   (Suggesting moderate to heavy reliance on context, typical of beginning readers)

Word	Isolation	Context
of	DK	of
the	the	the
when	where	when
were	where	were
(etc.)		

Example   (Suggesting little reliance on context and movement toward automatic decoding)

Word	Isolation	Context
of	of	of
the	the	the
when	when	when
were	were	were
(etc.)		

PART

2

TEACHER'S RECORDING FORMS
Word Lists

GRADED WORD LISTS

Summary of Directions

Present the student's copy of the graded words lists, starting with a list at least two grades below the student's current grade level (if more severe reading disability is suspected, begin as low as seems appropriate). Say, *"Pronounce each word for me. If you are not sure or do not know the word, at least tell me what you think it is."* Record all responses on this form. Have the student read from increasingly difficult lists until he or she misses at least three words on one of the lists.

Independent level = 0–1 error on a list
Instructional level = 2–4 errors on a list
Frustration level = 5 or more errors on a list

TEACHER'S RECORDING FORM

Word Card A		Word Card B	
Pre-Primer	*Primer*	*Grade 1*	*Grade 2*
1. be	1. car	1. are	1. our
2. play	2. new	2. is	2. way
3. a	3. not	3. by	3. town
4. you	4. with	4. when	4. send
5. can	5. help	5. jump	5. wide
6. he	6. her	6. how	6. young
7. look	7. up	7. night	7. early
8. run	8. come	8. today	8. believe
9. said	9. work	9. would	9. straight
10. here	10. this	10. thank	10. people
11. but	11. some	11. which	11. between
12. did	12. now	12. spring	12. thought
13. the	13. took	13. something	13. already
14. big	14. been	14. where	14. children
15. man	15. take	15. school	15. point

Number Missed: _____ _____ _____ _____

TEACHER'S RECORDING FORM

Word Card C

Grade 3	Grade 4	Grade 5
1. city _____	1. decided _____	1. cruel _____
2. moment _____	2. wrecked _____	2. kerosene _____
3. middle _____	3. served _____	3. business _____
4. frightened _____	4. pint _____	4. melted _____
5. different _____	5. amazed _____	5. develop _____
6. move _____	6. silent _____	6. abolish _____
7. several _____	7. letter _____	7. considered _____
8. exclaimed _____	8. study _____	8. especially _____
9. drew _____	9. realized _____	9. discussed _____
10. since _____	10. improved _____	10. furious _____
11. ground _____	11. flattered _____	11. stirred _____
12. enough _____	12. entered _____	12. splendid _____
13. brought _____	13. beauty _____	13. acquainted _____
14. though _____	14. coffin _____	14. grim _____
15. rough _____	15. Mrs. _____	15. ignore _____

Number Missed: _____   _____   _____

TEACHER'S RECORDING FORM

Word Card D

Grade 6	*Grade 7*	*Grade 8*
1. bridge _____	1. amber _____	1. universal _____
2. luxurious _____	2. nuclear _____	2. legislator _____
3. commercial _____	3. dominion _____	3. limitation _____
4. remained _____	4. manual _____	4. pretext _____
5. hysterical _____	5. sundry _____	5. persuasive _____
6. apparatus _____	6. reformatory _____	6. intrigue _____
7. ventured _____	7. capillary _____	7. flourish _____
8. generation _____	8. parson _____	8. pavilion _____
9. comment _____	9. blight _____	9. immaculate _____
10. biographer _____	10. mockery _____	10. acquired _____
11. necessity _____	11. wrestle _____	11. lyric _____
12. society _____	12. mission _____	12. entrust _____
13. caravan _____	13. satisfy _____	13. navigator _____
14. relativity _____	14. scripture _____	14. terrified _____
15. dainty _____	15. century _____	15. reputation _____

**Number
Missed:** _____   _____   _____

TEACHER'S RECORDING FORM

Word Card E

Grade 9	*Grade 10*	*Grade 11*
1. fascinating _____	1. persistent _____	1. galore _____
2. conscientious _____	2. adorn _____	2. abdicate _____
3. isolation _____	3. strenuous _____	3. rotunda _____
4. adolescence _____	4. baroness _____	4. cahoots _____
5. descendants _____	5. nausea _____	5. capitalism _____
6. molecule _____	6. desegregate _____	6. cantankerous _____
7. emissary _____	7. limerick _____	7. prevaricate _____
8. ritual _____	8. linguist _____	8. debutante _____
9. fortification _____	9. lore _____	9. effigy _____
10. momentous _____	10. aspen _____	10. exonerate _____
11. illuminate _____	11. lynch _____	11. gaudy _____
12. vulnerable _____	12. amnesty _____	12. cantilever _____
13. moccasins _____	13. malcontent _____	13. piebald _____
14. kinship _____	14. barometer _____	14. dastard _____
15. hideous _____	15. carnivorous _____	15. crunch _____

Number
Missed: _____   _____   _____

Form A Passages

GRADE 1 PASSAGE FORM A: TEACHER'S RECORDING FORM

PRIOR KNOWLEDGE

Do you like making things? _____

Do you paint pictures at school? _____

Can you tell me what a mobile is? _____

Now you are going to read a part of a story about an artist. Then I will ask you some questions about what you have read and what you thought about it.

Alexander Calder

Alexander Calder was a great artist. He

started making things <u>when</u> ₁ <u>he</u> ₚₚ was five.

Alexander's mother and father were artists,

too. They were happy that their son liked to

make things.

Many people know and love Alexander

Calder's art <u>today</u> ₁. He is best known for making

mobiles, a <u>new</u> ₚ kind of hanging art.

Notes:

Reading Time = ___ min. ___ sec. = ___ sec.   Words per Minute = 3,180 ÷ ___ sec. = ____ WPM

EJ   How much do you think you would enjoy reading the rest of this story? Point to the picture that is closest to the way you feel.

Show student the "rating card" reproduced here. Briefly review the meaning of each choice, and circle the number of the student's choice. Then, on the questions that follow, you may indicate the "value" of responses by recording a "–" for responses that are clearly incongruent, or illogical, or a "+" for any that are exceptionally full or detailed.

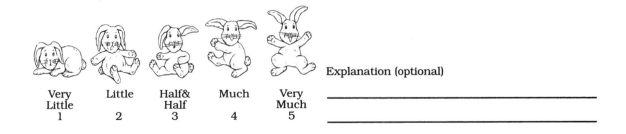

Very Little	Little	Half& Half	Much	Very Much
1	2	3	4	5

Explanation (optional)

_____

_____

READING THE LINES

> *Score:* **0** for incorrect, **1** for correct
> *Value:* – for incongruent, + for congruent

		Score	Value

F   1. At what age did Alexander start making things? (*when he was five years old*)

_____   _____   _____

F   2. What did Alexander's parents do? (*they were artists*)

_____   _____   _____

F   3. What is Alexander's last name? (*Calder*)

_____   _____   _____

V   4. What is a mobile? (*type of hanging art*)

_____   _____   _____

F   5. What is Alexander most known for today? (*making mobiles—a new kind hanging art*)

_____   _____   _____

READING BETWEEN THE LINES

		Score	Value

I   6. Do you think Alexander's parents liked being artists? (*yes—they must have liked it if they wanted their son to be one, too*)

_____   _____   _____

I   7. Why do you think Alexander's parents were happy that he liked to make things when he was a child? (*they probably hoped he would grow up to be an artist*)

_____   _____   _____

I   8. What do you think the rest of this story will be about? (*how Alexander grew up to be an artist*)

_____   _____   _____

CE   9. Tell how much you agree with this statement: "Being an artist would probably be an easy life." Point to the picture that shows the way you feel (answer should indicate that it might be fun to be an artist, but there might be difficulties too).

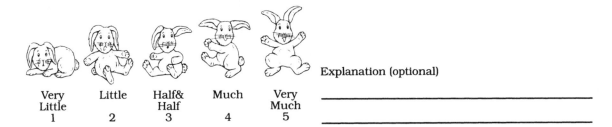

Very Little	Little	Half& Half	Much	Very Much
1	2	3	4	5

Explanation (optional)

_____

_____

Scoring Guide—Alexander Calder

Level	Word Recognition Errors	Comprehension Errors (Questions 1–9)
IND	0–1	0–1
INS	2–3	2
INS/FRU	4–6	3–4
FRU	7+	5+

Comp. % (Lines + Between)	
Errors	%
0	100
1	89
2	78
3	67
4	56
5	45
6	33
7	22
8	11
9	0

M   10. How well do you think you answered these questions so far? Point to the picture that is closest to the way you think you answered.

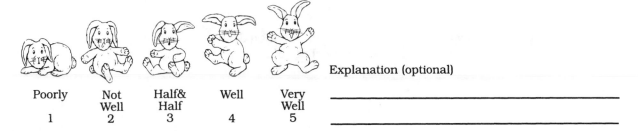

Poorly	Not Well	Half& Half	Well	Very Well
1	2	3	4	5

Explanation (optional)

_____

_____

READING BEYOND THE LINES

Score: **0** for unacceptable, **1** for acceptable

Score

AC   12. What does it take to be an artist? (*desire, talent, hard work, instruction*)

_____   _____

AC   13.   There are many kinds of art; music, painting, plays, and poems are some examples. What are some reasons why people *like* art? (*it offers a means of expression, it makes one feel it influences and pleases others, it can live on long after the artist is gone*)

_____   _____

M   14.   How well do you think you answered these last two questions? Point to the picture that is closest to the way you feel.

Poorly	Not Well	Half& Half	Well	Very Well
1	2	3	4	5

Explanation (optional)

_____

_____

OE   15.   Pretend you are an artist. Describe something people are doing in a home that you could paint a picture of. (*Answers will vary. Look for evidence of a creative perspective to the otherwise mundane. Also consider possible deeper meanings or psychological implications.*)

Score

Oral Response Notes:

_____   _____

_____

Optional: Following initial discussion of question 15, ask the student to write his or her answer on a separate sheet of paper. Attach this writing sample to the test materials, and record the student's score here.   _____

GRADE 2 PASSAGE FORM A: TEACHER'S RECORDING FORM

PRIOR KNOWLEDGE

Do you know what a crab is? _____

How do crabs walk? _____

Can you tell me what *fault* means? _____

Now you are going to read a story about a mother crab and her son. Then I will ask you some questions about what you have read and what you thought about it.

The Crab and His Mother	Notes:

An Old Crab said to <u>her</u> _P son, "Why do <u>you</u> _{PP}

walk sideways like that, my son? You ought to

walk <u>straight</u> ₂." <u>The</u> _{PP} <u>Young</u> ₂ Crab replied, "Show

me <u>how</u> ₁, dear mother, and I'll follow your

example." The Old Crab tried and tried, but then

she saw how foolish she had been to find fault

<u>with</u> _P her child.

Reading Time = ___ min. ___ sec. = ___ sec.   Words per Minute = 3,360 ÷ ___ sec. = _____ WPM

EJ   How much did you enjoy this story? Point to the picture that is closest to the way you feel.

> Show student the "rating card" reproduced here. Briefly review the meaning of each choice, and circle the number of the student's choice. Then, on the questions that follow, you may indicate the "value" of responses by recording a "–" for responses that are clearly incongruent, or illogical, or a "+" for any that are exceptionally full or detailed.

Very Little 1	Little 2	Half& Half 3	Much 4	Very Much 5	Explanation (optional)

_____

_____

READING THE LINES

> *Score:* **0** for incorrect, **1** for correct
> *Value:* **–** for incongruent, **+** for congruent

                                                                    Score   *Value*

F   1. How did the young crab walk? (*sideways*)

    _____   _____   _____

F   2. Complete this sentence: The Old Crab asked her son to walk
        _____. (*straight*)

    _____   _____   _____

F   3. What did the young crab say to his mother when his mother asked
        him to walk straight? (*show me how, dear mother, and I'll follow
        your example*)

    _____   _____   _____

V   4. What does the word "straight" mean in this passage? (*properly,
        frontwards*)

    _____   _____   _____

READING BETWEEN THE LINES

                                                                    Score   *Value*

I   5. Why wasn't the mother crab able to show her son how to walk
        straight? (*because all crabs walk sideways*)

    _____   _____   _____

I   6. Why would the mother crab even ask her son why he walked side-
        ways? (*to draw his attention to it, so he would try to change*)

    _____   _____   _____

I   7. How do you suppose the young crab's uncle walked? (*sideways*)

    _____   _____   _____

Scoring Guide—The Crab and His Mother		
Level	Word Recognition Errors	Comprehension Errors (Questions 1–7)
IND	0–1	0–1
INS	2–3	2
INS/FRU	4–6	3
FRU	7+	4+

Comp. % (Lines + Between)	
Errors	%
0	100
1	86
2	71
3	57
4	43
5	29
6	14
7	0

M 8. How well do you think you answered these questions? Point to the picture that is closest to the way you think you answered.

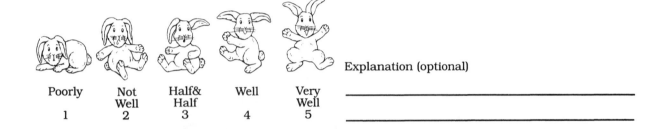

Poorly	Not Well	Half& Half	Well	Very Well
1	2	3	4	5

Explanation (optional)

_____

_____

READING BEYOND THE LINES

Score: **0** for unacceptable, **1** for acceptable

Score

CE 9. Why would the mother want her son to walk straight?

_____   _____

CE 10. Which statement do you think says the meaning of this story best, and why? (*Repeat items if necessary*)

_____ A. We learn best by examples.   (*best*)

_____ B. Listen to your mother, no matter what.   (*correct/irrelevant*)

_____ C. The things that are wrong with a child   (*simple/emotional*)
          are usually wrong with the parents.

Explanation: _____

_____

M 11. How well do you think you answered these related questions? Point to the picture that is closest to the way you feel.

Poorly	Not Well	Half& Half	Well	Very Well	Explanation (optional)
1	2	3	4	5	

OE 13. Do you think parents should point out their children's faults? Why or why not?

Score

Oral Response Notes:

Optional: Following initial discussion of question 13, ask the student to write his or her answer on a separate sheet of paper. Attach this writing sample to the test materials, and record the student's score here.

GRADE 3 PASSAGE FORM A: TEACHER'S RECORDING FORM

PRIOR KNOWLEDGE

Why is it hard for things to live in the desert? _____

Do you know of any things that live in the desert? _____

Can you tell me about a cactus? _____

Now you are going to read part of an article about the desert. Then I will ask you some questions about what you have read and what you thought about it.

The Desert: What Lives There	*Notes:*

The _pp_ desert is _1_ a place that gets very little rainfall. The ground _3_ is often sandy and rocky. When _1_ the sun beats down, the sand and rocks grow hot and dry. It is hard to imagine that a place like this is full of living things.

All living things need food, water, and some _p_ kind of shelter to survive. Some plants and animals are well suited to survive in the desert. They can _pp_ live off the food, water, and shelter that are _1_ there.

The cactus is one kind of plant that is suited to survive in the desert. The cactus has a special way _2_ of getting water in the dry desert soil. It spreads its roots out close to the top of the ground. When _1_ rain comes, the cactus roots soak up _p_ the water quickly before it drains deep into the sand.

Once a cactus plant gets water, it can store it for the dry days ahead. A cactus can store enough _3_ water from one rainstorm to last a long time.

Reading Time = ___ min. ___ sec. = ___ sec.   Words per Minute = 10,200 ÷ ___ sec. = _____ WPM

EJ   How much do you think you would enjoy reading the rest of this selection? Point to the picture that is closest to the way you feel.

Show student the "rating card" reproduced here. Briefly review the meaning of each choice, and circle the number of the student's choice. Then, on the questions that follow, you may indicate the "value" of responses by recording a "**–**" for responses that are clearly incongruent, or illogical, or a "**+**" for any that are exceptionally full or detailed.

Very Little	Little	Half& Half	Much	Very Much
1	2	3	4	5

Explanation (optional)

_____

_____

READING THE LINES

Score: **0** for incorrect, **1** for correct
Value: **–** for incongruent, **+** for congruent

			Score	Value

F   1. What is the ground like in the desert? (*sandy and rocky*)

F   2. According to the passage, what do all living things need to survive? (*food, water, and shelter*)

F   3. According to the passage, do many things live in the desert? (*yes— the passage says the desert is full of living things*)

CBF 4. How does a cactus plant get water in the desert soil? (*it spreads its roots out close to the top of the ground—when the rain comes, the cactus roots soak up all the water they can*)

V   5. What does the word "shelter" mean in this passage? (*protection*)

V   6. What does the word "survive" mean in this passage? (*to live on where other things have died, to have found a way to live in a different circumstance*)

_____   _____   _____

READING BETWEEN THE LINES

Score   Value

I   7. After reading this passage, do you think there are animals in the desert? (*yes—the passage says that the desert is full of living things; there probably are animals as well as plants*)

_____   _____   _____

I   8. What do you think the rest of this article will be about? (*other plants and animals that are able to live in the desert*)

_____   _____   _____

Scoring Guide—The Desert: What Lives There		
Level	Word Recognition Errors	Comprehension Errors (Questions 1–8)
IND	0–2	0–1
INS	3–8	2
INS/FRU	9–16	3–4
FRU	17+	5+

Comp. % (Lines + Between)	
Errors	%
0	100
1	88
2	75
3	63
4	50
5	38
6	25
7	13
8	0

M   9. How well do you think you answered these factual and thought questions? Point to the picture that is closest to the way you think you answered.

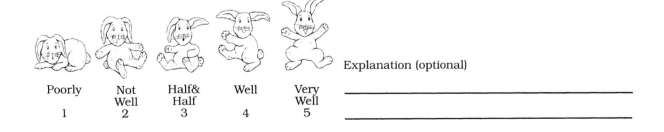

Poorly	Not Well	Half& Half	Well	Very Well
1	2	3	4	5

Explanation (optional)

_____

_____

READING BEYOND THE LINES

> *Score:* **0** for unacceptable, **1** for acceptable

CE 10. Tell how much you agree with this statement—*"It would probably be easy for a person to live in the desert."* Point to the picture that shows the way you feel. (*the explanation should indicate that it would be* possible *for a person to live in the desert, but that it would be difficult—we are not built for it, but we can find and make food and shelter*)

Explanation (optional)

Very Little 1	Little 2	Half& Half 3	Much 4	Very Much 5

_____

_____

Score

PS 11. The passage says that all living things need shelter, or protection. How do you think desert plants get protection from the sun and the wind? (*they may have tough, thick skins*)

_____   _____

PS 12. Name some things that you think would make it possible for people to live comfortably in the desert. (*shelter from the sun, means of storing water, etc.*)

_____   _____

AR 13. In what ways are deserts like oceans? (*they are both large areas where only certain living things can survive*)

_____   _____

AR 14. What do you suppose it would take for an animal to survive in a very *cold* place? (*some means of retaining heat, such as fur, or the availability of shelter*)

_____   _____

M 15. How well do you think you answered these related questions? Point to the picture that is closest to the way you feel.

Explanation (optional)

Poorly 1	Not Well 2	Half& Half 3	Well 4	Very Well 5

_____

_____

OE 16. Pretend that a cactus plant, an oak tree, and a jungle vine found themselves in the same place. Where might they be, and what might they say to one another?

Score

Oral Response Notes:

_____ _____

_____

Optional: Following initial discussion of question 16, ask the student to write his or her answer on a separate sheet of paper. Attach this writing sample to the test materials, and record the student's score here. _____

GRADE 4 PASSAGE FORM A: TEACHER'S RECORDING FORM

PRIOR KNOWLEDGE

Which is more attractive, a fox or a crow? _____

Which one do people think is more clever? _____

What does "flatter" mean? _____

Now you are going to read a story about a cunning fox. Then I will ask you some questions about what you have read and what you thought about it.

The Fox and the Crow

Notes:

A Crow was sitting on a branch of a tree with $_p$ a piece of cheese in her $_p$ beak when $_1$ a Fox observed her and set his brain to work $_p$ to discover some way of getting the cheese. Coming and standing under the $_{pp}$ tree, he $_{pp}$ looked up and said, "What a noble bird I see above me! Her beauty $_4$ is without equal; the hue of her plumage is rare. If only her voice were as sweet as her looks are lovely, she surely should be Queen of the Birds." The Crow was very flattered $_4$ by this, and just to show the Fox that she could sing, she gave a loud caw. Down came the cheese, of course, and the Fox, snatching it up $_p$, said, "You have a voice, madam, but what you don't have are $_1$ brains."

Reading Time = ___ min. ___ sec. = ___ sec. Words per Minute = 8,100 ÷ ___ sec. = ____ WPM

EJ   How much did you enjoy this story? Point to the picture that is closest to the way you feel.

> Show student the "rating card" reproduced here. Briefly review the meaning of each choice, and circle the number of the student's choice. Then, on the questions that follow, you may indicate the "value" of responses by recording a "–" for responses that are clearly incongruent, or illogical, or a "+" for any that are exceptionally full or detailed.

Very Little 1	Little 2	Half& Half 3	Much 4	Very Much 5	Explanation (optional)

_____

_____

READING THE LINES

> *Score:* **0** for incorrect, **1** for correct
> *Value:* **–** for incongruent, **+** for congruent

		Score	Value

F   1. Where was the crow? (*on the branch of a tree*)

_____   _____   _____

F   2. What did the fox want? (*the cheese in the crow's beak*)

_____   _____   _____

F   3. What did the fox use to get the cheese from the crow? (*the fox used his wits—he tricked her—flattery*)

_____   _____   _____

V   4. What does the word "flatter" mean? (*to overpraise, or to praise falsely*)

_____   _____   _____

V   5. What do you think the word "plumage" means in this passage? (*feathers*)

_____   _____   _____

READING BETWEEN THE LINES

Score   *Value*

I 6. What did the fox really mean when he said, "You have a voice, madam, but what you don't have are brains"? (*you are a fool / dumb / "get smart"*)

_____   _____   _____

AR 7. What is the lesson of this story? (*be careful of those who would flatter you*)

_____   _____   _____

Scoring Guide—The Fox and the Crow		
Level	Word Recognition Errors	Comprehension Errors (Questions 1–7)
IND	0–2	0–1
INS	3–7	2
INS/FRU	8–13	3
FRU	14+	4+

Comp. % (Lines + Between)	
Errors	%
0	100
1	86
2	71
3	57
4	43
5	29
6	14
7	0

M 8. How well do you think you answered these questions? Point to the picture that is closest to the way you think you answered.

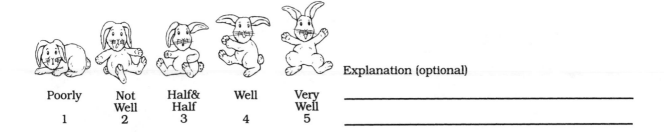

Poorly	Not Well	Half& Half	Well	Very Well
1	2	3	4	5

Explanation (optional)

_____

_____

READING BEYOND THE LINES

Score: **0** for unacceptable, **1** for acceptable

Score

CE 9. How do talk-show hosts and news people often get famous people to tell them things they otherwise would not? (*by flattering them*)

_____   _____

M 10. How well do you think you answered this related question? Point to the picture that is closest to the way you feel.

Explanation (optional)

Poorly	Not Well	Half& Half	Well	Very Well
1	2	3	4	5

_____

_____

OE 11. In your opinion, is flattery a good thing or a bad thing?

Score

Oral Response Notes:

_____ _____

_____

Optional: Following initial discussion of question 11, ask the student to write his or her answer on a separate sheet of paper. Attach this writing sample to the test materials, and record the student's score here. _____

PRIOR KNOWLEDGE

If you had to choose between farming or fishing, in which way would you rather make a living?

_____

How does a volcano work? _____

What is a tidal wave? _____

Now you are going to read the beginning of a longer story about a boy who lived in Japan. Then I will ask you some questions about what you have read and what you thought about it.

The Big Wave

Notes:

Kino lived on a farm. The farm lay on the side of a mountain in Japan. The fields were terraced by walls of stone, each one of them like a broad step up the mountain.

Above all the fields stood the farmhouse that was Kino's home. Sometimes he felt the climb was a hard one, <u>especially</u> $_5$ when he had been working in the lowest field and he wanted his supper. But after he had eaten each night and each morning, he was glad that he lived so high up, because he could look down on the broad blue ocean at the foot of the mountain.

The mountain rose so steeply out of the ocean that there was only a strip of sandy shore at its foot. Upon this strip was the small fishing village where Kino's good friend Jiya lived.

On days when the sky was bright and the winds mild, the ocean lay so calm and blue that it was hard to believe that it could ever be <u>cruel</u> $_5$ and angry. Yet even Kino never quite forgot that when he dived down under the warm blue surface, the water was cold and green. When the sun shone, the deep water was still. But when the deep water moved and heaved and <u>stirred</u> ₅, ah, then Kino was glad that his father was a farmer and not a fisherman.

And yet, one day, it was the earth that brought the big wave. Deep under the ocean, fires raged in the heart of the earth. The icy cold of the water could not chill those fires. Rocks were <u>melted</u> ₅ and boiled, but they could not break through the crust of the ocean's bed. At last the steam grew so strong that it forced its way through to the mouth of the far-off volcano.

Reading Time = ___ min. ___ sec. = ___ sec.   Words per Minute = 18,060 ÷ ___ sec. = _____ WPM

EJ   How much do you think you would enjoy reading the rest of this selection? Point to the picture that is closest to the way you feel.

Show student the "rating card" reproduced here. Briefly review the meaning of each choice, and circle the number of the student's choice. Then, on the questions that follow, you may indicate the "value" of responses by recording a "–" for responses that are clearly incongruent, or illogical, or a "+" for any that are exceptionally full or detailed.

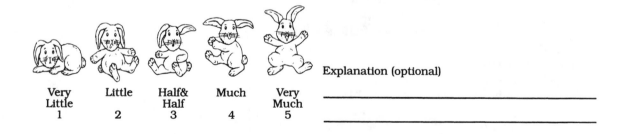

| Very Little | Little | Half& Half | Much | Very Much |
| 1 | 2 | 3 | 4 | 5 |

Explanation (optional)

_____

_____

READING THE LINES

> *Score:* **0** for incorrect, **1** for correct
> *Value:* – for incongruent, **+** for congruent

		Score	Value

F   1.   What country does Kino live in? (*Japan*)

_____   _____   _____

F   2.   What does Kino's father do? (*he is a farmer*)

_____   _____   _____

F   3.   How could a farm be built on the side of a mountain? (*in narrow strips of land, like steps*)

_____   _____   _____

F   4.   What is the name of Kino's good friend? (*Jiya*)

_____   _____   _____

V   5.   What does the word "heave" mean in this sentence: ". . . when the deep water moved and <u>heaved</u> and stirred . . ." (*raised, or lifted up*)

_____   _____   _____

READING BETWEEN THE LINES

		Score	Value

I   6.   Do you think Kino liked or feared the ocean? (*he both liked and feared it*)

_____   _____   _____

I   7.   Why was Kino glad that he was a farmer and not a fisherman? (*he was afraid of the ocean when the weather was bad*)

_____   _____   _____

I   8.   Do you think Kino's family uses large equipment to farm their land? Why or why not? (*no—it would be difficult to move large equipment on the narrow strips of land; or, because it sounds like they live a simple life*)

_____   _____   _____

I   9. What do you think will happen as this story continues? (*the big wave will come and damage the land*)

_____   ____   ___

Scoring Guide—The Big Wave		
Level	Word Recognition Errors	Comprehension Errors (Questions 1–9)
IND	0–3	0–1
INS	4–15	2
INS/FRU	16–29	3
FRU	30+	5+

Comp. % (Lines + Between)	
Errors	%
0	100
1	89
2	78
3	67
4	56
5	45
6	33
7	22
8	11
9	0

M   10. How well do you think you answered these questions? Point to the picture that is closest to the way you think you answered.

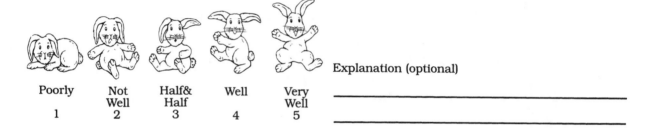

Poorly	Not Well	Half& Half	Well	Very Well
1	2	3	4	5

Explanation (optional)

_____

_____

READING BEYOND THE LINES

Score: **0** for unacceptable, **1** for acceptable

CE   11. Tell how much you agree with this statement—*"Oceans should be feared."* Point to the picture that shows the way you feel. (*the explanation should indicate that the ocean can be dangerous*)

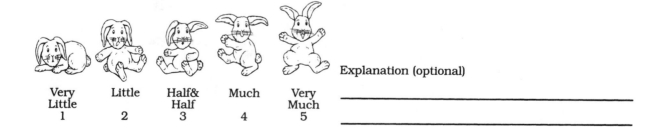

Very Little	Little	Half& Half	Much	Very Much
1	2	3	4	5

Explanation (optional)

_____

_____

Score

AR   12.   How are farmland and oceans alike? (*both provide food*)

_____   _____

PS   13.   What might be done to protect yourself from big waves and soil erosion? (*by being prepared—student should elaborate means*)

_____   _____

PS   14.   What might be done to keep the oceans and the land clean? (*pollution control, recycling, waste management, etc.*)

_____   _____

M   15.   How well do you think you answered these last three questions? Point to the picture that is closest to the way you feel.

Poorly	Not Well	Half& Half	Well	Very Well
1	2	3	4	5

Explanation (optional)

_____

_____

OE   16.   What might you do if you and your family owned some very good farm land, but on occasion it would flood over from heavy rains and wipe out your home and most of your possessions?

Score

Oral Response Notes:

_____   _____

_____

Optional: Following initial discussion of question 16, ask the student to write his or her answer on a separate sheet of paper. Attach this writing sample to the test materials, and record the student's score here.   _____

PRIOR KNOWLEDGE

What do you think frogs are afraid of? _____

What is a stork? _____

Who was Jupiter? _____

Now you are going to read a story about frogs. Then I will ask you some questions about what you have read and what you thought about it.

The Frogs Who Wanted a King

Notes:

Time was when the Frogs were discontented because they had no one to rule over them. So the Frogs sent a representative to Jupiter to ask him to give them a king.

Jupiter, despising the folly of their request, cast a log into the pool where they lived. He said, "Here, this log will be your king." The Frogs were terrified at first by the splash and scuttled away into the deepest parts of the pool; but

by and by, when they saw that the log remained [6] motionless, one by one they ventured [6] to the surface again, and before long, growing bolder, they began to feel such contempt for it that they even took to sitting upon it. Thinking that a king of that sort was an insult to their dignity, they sent another message to Jupiter, begging him to take away the sluggish king he had given them and to give them a better one. Jupiter, annoyed at being pestered in this way, sent a stork to rule over them, who no sooner than he arrived among them began to catch and eat the Frogs as fast as he could.

Reading Time = ___ min. ___ sec. = ___ sec.   Words per Minute = 11,340 ÷ ___ sec. = ____ WPM

EJ   How much did you enjoy this story? Point to the picture that is closest to the way you feel.

Show student the "rating card" reproduced here. Briefly review the meaning of each choice, and circle the number of the student's choice. Then, on the questions that follow, you may indicate the "value" of responses by recording a "−" for responses that are clearly incongruent, or illogical, or a "+" for any that are exceptionally full or detailed.

| Very Little 1 | Little 2 | Half& Half 3 | Much 4 | Very Much 5 |

Explanation (optional)

_____

_____

READING THE LINES

Score: **0** for incorrect, **1** for correct
Value: **−** for incongruent, **+** for congruent

                                                                    Score   *Value*

F   1. Why did the frogs first send a messenger to Jupiter? (*to ask him to give them a king*)

_____   _____   _____

F   2. Were they satisfied with the king? Why? (*no, it was only a log*)

_____   _____   _____

F   3. What did the frogs do when they were dissatisfied with their king? (*they sent Jupiter a second message; asked for a new king*)

_____   _____   _____

F   4. How did Jupiter punish the frogs for bothering him a second time? (*he sent a stork to rule over them—the stork caught and ate them as fast as he could*)

_____   _____   _____

V   5. What does the word "discontented" mean in this passage? (*dissatisfied; unhappy*)

_____   _____   _____

READING BETWEEN THE LINES

Score   Value

I   6. Who was Jupiter? (*the frogs' god*)

_____   _____   _____

I   7. Why did Jupiter toss a log into the frogs' pool and say that that should be their king? (*to show them that their request was foolish*)

_____   _____   _____

I   8. Why did the frogs think that the log king was an insult to their dignity? (*the king should be superior to them—he should be active, intelligent and have authority—but the log was motionless and stupid*)

_____   _____   _____

I   9. Do you think that, if the story continued, the frogs would ask Jupiter for a third king? (*no—they probably had learned to stop making unnecessary requests or there would be no frogs left*)

_____   _____   _____

Scoring Guide—The Frogs Who Wanted a King		
Level	Word Recognition Errors	Comprehension Errors (Questions 1–9)
IND	0–2	0–1
INS	3–10	2
INS/FRU	11–18	3–4
FRU	19+	5+

Comp. % (Lines + Between)	
Errors	%
0	100
1	89
2	78
3	67
4	56
5	45
6	33
7	22
8	11
9	0

M   10. How well do you think you answered these factual and thought questions? Point to the picture that is closest to the way you think you answered.

Poorly	Not Well	Half& Half	Well	Very Well
1	2	3	4	5

Explanation (optional)

_____

READING BEYOND THE LINES

> *Score:* **0** for unacceptable, **1** for acceptable

Score

CE 11. Do you think the frogs were right in asking for a king? (*they were very stupid to ask for an absolute ruler or king*)

_____   _____

AC 12. What have you learned from this story? (*be your own ruler; don't make unnecessary requests*)

_____   _____

FK 13. How do you feel when you meet something or someone you don't know for the first time? (*answers will vary; probe for explanation*)

_____   _____

M 14. How well do you think you answered these last three questions? Point to the picture that is closest to the way you feel.

Poorly	Not Well	Half& Half	Well	Very Well
1	2	3	4	5

Explanation (optional)

_____

_____

OE 15. Which would you rather *have*: a leader or a ruler? Why?

Score

Oral Response Notes:

_____   _____

_____

Optional: Following initial discussion of question 15, ask the student to write his or her answer on a separate sheet of paper. Attach this writing sample to the test materials, and record the student's score here.   _____

GRADE 7 PASSAGE FORM A: TEACHER'S RECORDING FORM

PRIOR KNOWLEDGE

Do you know any economic uses of whales? _____

How did men hunt whales? _____

Can you describe a whale? _____

Now you are going to read the beginning of a longer article about whaling. Then I will ask you some questions about what you have read and what you thought about it.

Whaling	Notes:

Whaling

Before the discovery of oil in the ground, oil from whales was used to lubricate the wheels of machinery and to fuel lamps. Whalebone was used in the nineteenth <u>century</u> ₇ for a number of practical and decorative household items. It was also an important part of women's wardrobes in the days when corsets and hoop skirts were worn.

As more and more ships hunted whales to <u>satisfy</u> ₇ a growing market for whale oil and bone, trips grew longer and longer. Rather than spend a morning rowing a boat from the beach, nineteenth-century whalers took ships around the world on hunts that lasted for years. Trips three to five years long were common. Once home, a whaling man stopped barely long enough to see his children before he was off to sea again. The risks of whaling were such that the odds were two to one against any sailors returning from such a trip.

Reading Time = ___ min. ___ sec. = ___ sec.   Words per Minute = 9,180 ÷ ___ sec. = _____ WPM

EJ   How much do you think you would enjoy reading the rest of this selection? Point to the picture that is closest to the way you feel.

Show student the "rating card" reproduced here. Briefly review the meaning of each choice, and circle the number of the student's choice. Then, on the questions that follow, you may indicate the "value" of responses by recording a "−" for responses that are clearly incongruent, or illogical, or a "+" for any that are exceptionally full or detailed.

| Very Little 1 | Little 2 | Half& Half 3 | Much 4 | Very Much 5 |

Explanation (optional)

_____

_____

READING THE LINES

Score: **0** for incorrect, **1** for correct
Value: **−** for incongruent, **+** for congruent

                                                                    Score   *Value*

F   1. According to this passage, when did people use oil from whales a lot? (*before the discovery of oil in the ground / nineteenth century*)

    _____   _____   _____

F   2. What were two economic uses of whales at that time? (*lubricate machines, fuel lamps, decorations, women's wear*)

    _____   _____   _____

F   3. How long did a whaling trip usually last in the nineteenth century? (*three to five years*)

    _____   _____   _____

F   4. Whaling was not very safe. What were the odds that a man would not return? (*2 to 1*)

    _____   _____   _____

V   5. What does the word "lubricate" mean in this passage? (*to grease or make slippery*)

    _____   _____   _____

READING BETWEEN THE LINES

Score   Value

I   6. Why did the trips for whaling grow longer and longer? (*the number
       of whales decreased, so they had to go farther to find them*)

_____   _____   _____

I   7. According to the *title* of the passage, what do you think the rest of
       this article will be about? (*hunting whales*)

_____   _____   _____

Scoring Guide—Whaling		
Level	Word Recognition Errors	Comprehension Errors (Questions 1–7)
IND	0–2	0–1
INS	3–8	2
INS/FRU	9–15	3
FRU	16+	4+

Comp. % (Lines + Between)	
Errors	%
0	100
1	86
2	71
3	57
4	43
5	29
6	14
7	0

M   8. How well do you think you answered these factual and thought questions? Point to the
       picture that is closest to the way you think you answered.

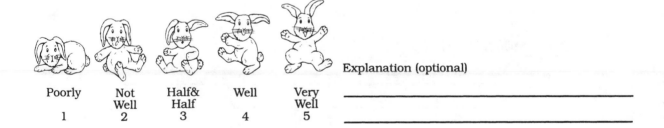

Poorly	Not Well	Half& Half	Well	Very Well
1	2	3	4	5

Explanation (optional)

_____

_____

READING BEYOND THE LINES

Score: **0** for unacceptable, **1** for acceptable

Score

SC   9. Do you suppose that whale oil is still used today? Why or why not? (*yes, but
        mostly outside the USA*)

_____   _____

SC 10. Is hunting whales still risky today? Why or why not? (*no—modern equipment and better ships make it safer*)

_____   _____

SC 11. Do people eat whales? If yes, who? (*probably, but it doesn't say; Eskimos*)

_____   _____

CE 12. To be a whaler, what qualities should one probably possess? (*strength, courage, endurance, patience*)

_____   _____

M 13. How well do you think you answered these last four questions? Point to the picture that is closest to the way you feel.

Poorly	Not Well	Half& Half	Well	Very Well	Explanation (optional)
1	2	3	4	5	_____

OE 14. Should whaling be outlawed? Why? (*yes—there are other ways to get oil and food*)

Score

Oral Response Notes:

_____   _____

_____

Optional: Following initial discussion of question 14, ask the student to write his or her answer on a separate sheet of paper. Attach this writing sample to the test materials, and record the student's score here.   _____

GRADE 8 PASSAGE FORM A: TEACHER'S RECORDING FORM

PRIOR KNOWLEDGE

Do you know anyone who is really good at promoting him- or herself? _____

What is an antidote? _____

What does a cobbler do? _____

Now you are going to read a story about a cobbler. Then I will ask you some questions about what you have read and what you thought about it.

The Cobbler Turned Doctor

Notes:

A very unskillful cobbler, finding himself unable to make a living at his trade, gave up mending boots and took to doctoring instead. He let it be known that he had the secret of a universal $_8$ antidote against all poisons, and he acquired $_8$ no small reputation $_8$, thanks to his talent for promoting $_8$ himself. One day, however, the cobbler-turned-doctor fell very ill, and the king of the country decided he would test the value of his remedy. Calling, therefore, for a cup, he poured out a dose of the antidote and, pretending to mix poison with it, really added a little water and commanded him to drink it. Terrified $_8$ by the fear of being poisoned, the cobbler confessed that he knew nothing about medicine and that his antidote was worthless. Then the king summoned his subjects and addressed them as follows: "What folly could be greater than yours? Here is this cobbler to whom no one will send his boots to be mended, and yet you have not hesitated to entrust him with your lives!"

Reading Time = ___ min. ___ sec. = ___ sec.   Words per Minute = 10,440 ÷ ___ sec. = _____ WPM

EJ   How much did you enjoy this story? Point to the picture that is closest to the way you feel.

> Show student the "rating card" reproduced here. Briefly review the meaning of each choice, and circle the number of the student's choice. Then, on the questions that follow, you may indicate the "value" of responses by recording a "**–**" for responses that are clearly incongruent, or illogical, or a "**+**" for any that are exceptionally full or detailed.

Very Little 1	Little 2	Half& Half 3	Much 4	Very Much 5

Explanation (optional)

_____

_____

READING THE LINES

> *Score:* **0** for incorrect, **1** for correct
> *Value:* **–** for incongruent, **+** for congruent

		Score	Value

F   1. Why did the cobbler change his trade? (*he wasn't good enough to make a living at it*)

_____   _____   _____

F   2. How did he acquire his reputation as a doctor? (*by promoting himself and by lying*)

_____   _____   _____

F   3. What happened to the cobbler one day? (*he became very ill*)

_____   _____   _____

F   4. How did the king test the value of the cobbler's medicine? (*he asked him to take his own medicine mixed with what the cobbler thought was poison*)

_____   _____   _____

V   5. What does the word "antidote" mean in this passage? (*a medicine that counteracts poison*)

_____   _____   _____

READING BETWEEN THE LINES

Score   Value

I   6. Did the king believe in the cobbler's antidote at first? Explain your
         answer. (*yes, he did, but had doubts, so he pretended to mix poison
         with the antidote and commanded the cobbler to drink it*)

         _____   _____ _____

         _____   _____ _____

I   7. What was the lesson that the king wished to give to his subjects?
         (*you shouldn't easily believe anything before you have proof—don't
         try to fool this wise, old king*)

         _____   _____ _____

         _____   _____ _____

Scoring Guide—The Cobbler Turned Doctor		
Level	Word Recognition Errors	Comprehension Errors (Questions 1–7)
IND	0–2	0–1
INS	3–9	2
INS/FRU	10–17	3
FRU	18+	4+

Comp. % (Lines + Between)	
Errors	%
0	100
1	86
2	71
3	57
4	43
5	29
6	14
7	0

M   8. How well do you think you answered these factual and thought questions? Point to the
         picture that is closest to the way you think you answered.

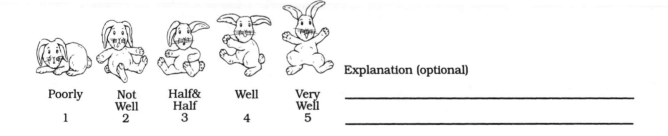

Poorly	Not Well	Half& Half	Well	Very Well	Explanation (optional)
1	2	3	4	5	_____

_____

READING BEYOND THE LINES

> *Score:* **0** for unacceptable, **1** for acceptable

Score

CE 9. Why did people believe in the cobbler's antidote so easily? (*when someone is ill, they're vulnerable and willing to try almost anything*)

_____   _____

CE 10. How would you describe the king? (What were some of his traits or characteristics?) (*wise, strong leader, concerned*)

_____   _____

EV 11. What should you do if someone recommends a cure to you? (*ask for proof of its value / check-up on its value*)

_____   _____

M 12. How well do you think you answered these related questions? Point to the picture that is closest to the way you feel.

Poorly	Not Well	Half& Half	Well	Very Well
1	2	3	4	5

Explanation (optional)

_____

_____

OE 13. Can you explain the difference between being "cynical" and being "skeptical"?

Score

Oral Response Notes:

_____   _____

_____

Optional: Following initial discussion of question 13, ask the student to write his or her answer on a separate sheet of paper. Attach this writing sample to the test materials, and record the student's score here.   _____

GRADE 9 PASSAGE FORM A: TEACHER'S RECORDING FORM

PRIOR KNOWLEDGE

Do you think storytelling requires special skills? _____

Do you know anyone who can really tell a story well? _____

What kind of boats did Indians use? _____

Now you are going to read the beginning of a passage about a storyteller. Then I will ask you some questions about what you have read and what you thought about it.

James Houston:
Tales of the Far North

Notes:

Storytelling is an ancient art that all peoples have used to pass on information and to keep the traditions of their society alive. Canadian-born James Houston is a modern-day master storyteller. He skillfully combines his own <u>fascinating</u> $_9$ stories of adventure with tales of the northern Canadian Indians and Eskimos. These tales have never before been written down.

When James Houston was very <u>young</u> $_2$, his father visited the American Indians of the prairies and the Far West almost every year and brought back gifts of beaded moosehide moccasins $_9$. Both Houston and his sister watched and listened as their father drew pictures and told them of the wonderful things he had seen.

The family spent many summers on Lake Simcoe in Ontario. There Houston met an old man who introduced the boy to his Ojibwa people. Sometimes the Ojibwa Indians would invite James to fish with them or to gather wild rice from their canoes. They lived in complete harmony with nature. The Ojibwa were not only a strong link with the past but also a strong influence on Houston's future.

Reading Time = ___ min. ___ sec. = ___ sec.   Words per Minute = 10,740 ÷ ___ sec. = ____ WPM

EJ   How much do you think you would enjoy reading the rest of this selection? Point to the picture that is closest to the way you feel.

Show student the "rating card" reproduced here. Briefly review the meaning of each choice, and circle the number of the student's choice. Then, on the questions that follow, you may indicate the "value" of responses by recording a "−" for responses that are clearly incongruent, or illogical, or a "+" for any that are exceptionally full or detailed.

| Very Little 1 | Little 2 | Half& Half 3 | Much 4 | Very Much 5 | Explanation (optional) |

_____

_____

READING THE LINES

Score: **0** for incorrect, **1** for correct
Value: **−** for incongruent, **+** for congruent

                                                         Score   *Value*

F   1.   According to this selection, what are the purposes of storytelling? (*to pass on information and keep the traditions alive*)

_____   ____   ____

F   2.   What makes James Houston a modern-day master storyteller? (*he skillfully combines his own fascinating stories of adventure with tales of the northern Canadian Indians and Eskimos*)

_____   ____   ____

F   3.   When James Houston was very young, what did his father do almost every year? (*visited the American Indians of the prairies and the Far West*)

_____   ____   ____

F   4.   Where did James' family often spend their summers? (*on Lake Simcoe in Ontario*)

_____   ____   ____

V 5. What does the word "harmony" mean in this passage? (*getting along together*)

_____ _____ _____

READING BETWEEN THE LINES

Score   Value

I 6. Do you think that Houston's father was also a good storyteller? Give reasons to support your answer. (*yes—both Houston and his sister were greatly attracted by their father's stories*)

_____ _____ _____

I 7. Where is Ontario, and how do you know that? (*in Canada; it is implied in the story, or I already knew that*)

_____ _____ _____

Scoring Guide—James Houston		
Level	Word Recognition Errors	Comprehension Errors (Questions 1–7)
IND	0–2	0–1
INS	3–9	2
INS/FRU	10–17	3
FRU	18+	4+

Comp. % (Lines + Between)	
Errors	%
0	100
1	86
2	71
3	57
4	43
5	29
6	14
7	0

M 8. How well do you think you answered these factual and thought questions? Point to the picture that is closest to the way you think you answered.

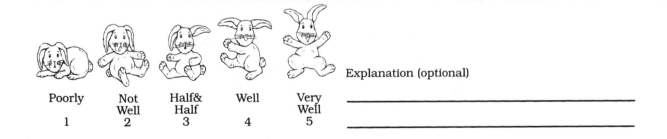

Poorly	Not Well	Half& Half	Well	Very Well	Explanation (optional)
1	2	3	4	5	_____

_____

READING BEYOND THE LINES

> *Score:* **0** for unacceptable, **1** for acceptable

Score

SC 9. Besides passing on information and keeping the traditions of the society, what is the other major purpose of storytelling? (*entertainment, education*)

_____ _____

CE 10. Who are *more* interested in listening to stories, children or adults? Why? (*children; they are more filled with wonder and need to learn*)

_____ _____

_____

_____

CE 11. What are qualities of a good storyteller? (*interesting person, good voice, dramatic*)

_____ _____

M 12. How well do you think you answered these last few questions? Point to the picture that is closest to the way you feel.

Poorly	Not Well	Half& Half	Well	Very Well
1	2	3	4	5

Explanation (optional)

_____

_____

OE 13. Briefly, tell me a story that comes to mind from when you were younger. Did it have a moral? What was the moral?

Score

Oral Response Notes:

_____ _____

_____

Optional: Following initial discussion of question 13, ask the student to write his or her answer on a separate sheet of paper. Attach this writing sample to the test materials, and record the student's score here. _____

Form B Passages

GRADE 1 PASSAGE FORM B: TEACHER'S RECORDING FORM

PRIOR KNOWLEDGE

How do people usually travel on or across water? _____

Who are Indians? _____

Do you know a name for an Indian boat? _____

Now you are going to listen to or read part of a story about how Indians lived and traveled. Then I will ask you some questions about what you have heard and what you thought about it.

A Better Way	**Notes:**
Long ago, many American Indians lived near water. They wanted to travel on the water. They wanted to travel fast. They also wanted to carry things with them when they traveled.	
The American Indians found a way to carry their things quickly over the water. They made a new kind of boat called a canoe.	

Reading Time = ___ min. ___ sec. = ___ sec.   Words per Minute = 3,300 ÷ ___ sec. = ____ WPM

EJ   How much do you think you would enjoy listening to the rest of this story? Point to the picture that is closest to the way you feel.

Show student the "rating card" reproduced here. Briefly review the meaning of each choice, and circle the number of the student's choice. Then on the questions that follow, you may indicate the "value" of responses by recording a "–" for responses that are clearly incongruent, or illogical, or a "+" for any that are exceptionally full or detailed.

Very Little 1	Little 2	Half& Half 3	Much 4	Very Much 5	Explanation (optional)
					_____
					_____

READING THE LINES

> *Score:* **0** for incorrect, **1** for correct
> *Value:* **–** for incongruent, **+** for congruent

                                                                    Score   *Value*

F   1. Who is this story about? (*American Indians*)

——————————————————————————— ——— ———

F   2. What did the Indians want to do on the water? (*to travel on the
          water, to go fast, and carry things with them*)

——————————————————————————— ——— ———

V   3. What does the word "canoe" mean in this passage? (*type of boat
          used by the Indians*)

——————————————————————————— ——— ———

READING BETWEEN THE LINES

                                                                    Score   *Value*

I   4. What do you think the rest of the story will be about? (*how Indians
          invented or made canoes*)

——————————————————————————— ——— ———

I   5. Why do you think that American Indians liked to live near water?
          (*so they could get to their boats easily, or so they could travel*)

——————————————————————————— ——— ———

I   6. Do you think that most Indians still travel by canoes today? (*no,
          probably not—the story said that it was long ago*)

——————————————————————————— ——— ———

Scoring Guide—A Better Way		
Level	Word Recognition Errors	Comprehension Errors (Questions 1–6)
IND	0–1	0
INS	2–3	1
INS/FRU	4–5	2
FRU	6+	3+

Comp. % (Lines + Between)	
Errors	%
0	100
1	83
2	66
3	50
4	33
5	17
6	0

M   7.   How well do you think you answered these questions? Point to the picture that is closest to the way you think you answered.

Poorly	Not Well	Half & Half	Well	Very Well
1	2	3	4	5

Explanation (optional)

_____

_____

READING BEYOND THE LINES

Score: **0** for unacceptable, **1** for acceptable

Score

FK   8.   How do we travel over water today? (*boats/bridges/airplanes/hovercraft, etc.*)

_____   _____

FK   9.   What did the Indians probably make their canoes from? (*wood; trees*)

_____   _____

M   10.   How well do you think you answered these last two questions? Point to the picture that is closest to the way you feel.

Poorly	Not Well	Half & Half	Well	Very Well
1	2	3	4	5

Explanation (optional)

_____

_____

OE   11.   Do you think that more people today should live like the American Indians did then? Why or why not? Tell me more about it.

Score

Oral Response Notes:

_____   _____

_____

Optional: Following initial discussion of question 11, ask the student to write his or her answer on a separate sheet of paper. Attach this writing sample to the test materials, and record the student's score here.   _____

GRADE 2 PASSAGE FORM B: TEACHER'S RECORDING FORM

PRIOR KNOWLEDGE

Which do you think is more frightening: a fox or a lion? Explain. _____

Which one is bigger? _____

Can you describe a lion? _____

Now you are going to listen to (or read) a story about a fox. Then I will ask you some questions about what you have heard and what you thought about it.

The Fox and the Lion

One day, a fox met a lion. The fox had never seen a lion before. The fox was terrified by the lion's large size and big mouth. He was ready to die with fear.

After a time he met the lion again and was still frightened, but not so much as he had been when he first met the lion.

When he saw the lion for the third time, he was far from being afraid. He went up and began to talk to the lion as if he had known the lion all his life.

Notes:

Reading Time = ___ min. ___ sec. = ___ sec. Words per Minute = 5,700 ÷ ___ sec. = _____ WPM

EJ   How much did you enjoy this story? Point to the picture that is closest to the way you feel.

Show student the "rating card" reproduced here. Briefly review the meaning of each choice, and circle the number of the student's choice. Then on the questions that follow, you may indicate the "value" of responses by recording a "–" for responses that are clearly incongruent, or illogical, or a "+" for any that are exceptionally full or detailed.

Very Little	Little	Half& Half	Much	Very Much
1	2	3	4	5

Explanation (optional)

_____

_____

123

READING THE LINES

> *Score:* **0** for incorrect, **1** for correct
> *Value:* **–** for incongruent, **+** for congruent

		Score	Value

F   1. How did the fox feel when he met the lion for the first time? (*he was afraid*)

_____   _____   _____

F   2. How did the fox feel when he met the lion a second time? (*he was not as afraid*)

_____   _____   _____

F   3. How many times did the fox and the lion meet in the story? (*three times*)

_____   _____   _____

V   4. What does the word "terrified" mean in this story? (*frightened, or very afraid*)

_____   _____   _____

READING BETWEEN THE LINES

		Score	Value

I   5. Why was the fox less frightened each time he met the lion? (*each time he met the lion, nothing happened; this made him think the lion was not to be feared*)

_____   _____   _____

I   6. Should the fox have stopped being afraid of the lion so soon? (*no*)

_____   _____   _____

Scoring Guide—The Fox and the Lion		
Level	Word Recognition Errors	Comprehension Errors (Questions 1–6)
IND	0–1	0
INS	2–5	1
INS/FRU	6–9	2
FRU	10+	3+

Comp. % (Lines + Between)	
Errors	%
0	100
1	83
2	66
3	50
4	33
5	17
6	0

M   7.   How well do you think you answered these factual and thought questions? Point to the picture that is closest to the way you think you answered.

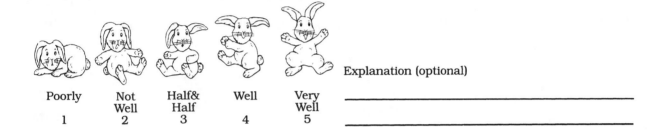

Poorly	Not Well	Half& Half	Well	Very Well	Explanation (optional)
1	2	3	4	5	_____

READING BEYOND THE LINES

> *Score:* **0** for unacceptable, **1** for acceptable

CE   8.   Tell how much you agree with this statement—"The fox should keep fearing the lion." Point to the picture that shows the way you feel. Explain why you think so. (*The explanation should indicate that the lion is still dangerous, even if he hasn't harmed the fox yet.*)

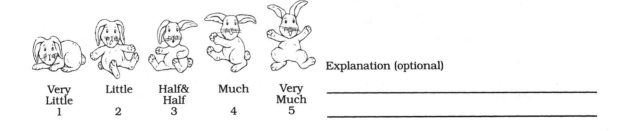

Very Little	Little	Half& Half	Much	Very Much	Explanation (optional)
1	2	3	4	5	_____

Score

SC   9. Why do you think that the lion did not eat the fox? (*the lion probably wasn't hungry, or other reasonable responses*)

_____   _____

SC   10. Do you suppose that there are some animals that might be afraid of a fox? (*yes*) Can you name some? (*answers that indicate small or defenseless animals*)

_____   _____

SC   11. What are some ways that animals have to keep from being hunted and killed by larger animals? (*some examples: make smells; run fast; hide in holes or in trees; play dead; have thorny or inedible skins*)

_____   _____

M   12. How well do you think you answered these last few questions? Point to the picture that is closest to the way you feel.

Poorly	Not Well	Half& Half	Well	Very Well
1	2	3	4	5

Explanation (optional)

_____

_____

OE   13. Is there something that you think you should fear?

Score

Oral Response Notes:

_____   _____

_____

Optional: Following initial discussion of question 13, ask the student to write his or her answer on a separate sheet of paper. Attach this writing sample to the test materials, and record the student's score here.   _____

GRADE 3 PASSAGE FORM B: TEACHER'S RECORDING FORM

PRIOR KNOWLEDGE

Have you ever flown a kite? If not, do you think you would like to? _____

How would someone who's fishing know there's a fish on the line? _____

What can you tell me about the Chinese? _____

Now you are going to listen to (or read) part of a story about how kites were used. Then I will ask you some questions about what you have heard and what you thought about it.

Kites in Flight

Did you know that people began flying kites more than two thousand years ago? The Chinese were the first people to invent and use kites. The kites they made were very beautiful. Some were shaped like fish, while others were made to look like dragons.

Sometimes the Chinese people flew kites just for fun. At other times they used kites to help them with their work. They tied a fishing line to the end of a kite. When a fish bit the bait, the kite moved. Then the kite and the fish were pulled in. Chinese farmers put kites in their fields to scare away birds that tried to eat their crops.

Notes:

Reading Time = ___ min. ___ sec. = ___ sec.   Words per Minute = 6,660 ÷ ___ sec. = ____ WPM

EJ   How much do you think you would enjoy listening to the rest of this story? Point to the picture that is closest to the way you feel.

Show student the "rating card" reproduced here. Briefly review the meaning of each choice, and circle the number of the student's choice. Then on the questions that follow, you may indicate the "value" of responses by recording a "–" for responses that are clearly incongruent, or illogical, or a "+" for any that are exceptionally full or detailed.

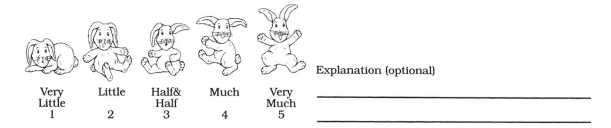

| Very Little 1 | Little 2 | Half& Half 3 | Much 4 | Very Much 5 |

Explanation (optional)

_____

_____

READING THE LINES

Score: **0** for incorrect, **1** for correct
Value: **–** for incongruent, **+** for congruent

| | *Score* | *Value* |

F   1. According to the story, when did people begin flying kites? (*more than two thousand years ago*)

_____   _____   _____

F   2. Who were the first people to use kites? (*the Chinese*)

_____   _____   _____

F   3 . Tell two ways that the Chinese used kites to help them with their work. (*they used kites for fishing and scaring away birds in the fields*)

_____   _____   _____

V   4. What does the word "invent" mean in this passage? (*create for the first time*)

_____   _____   _____

READING BETWEEN THE LINES

| | *Score* | *Value* |

I   5. How can a kite protect crops in a field? (*it is large; it might look like another bird; it is unfamiliar*)

_____   _____   _____

I 6. From the information in the passage, how can you tell that the Chinese enjoyed making and flying kites? (*the kites were beautifully made, and sometimes they flew them for fun*)

_____   _____   _____

Scoring Guide—Kites in Flight		
Level	Word Recognition Errors	Comprehension Errors (Questions 1–6)
IND	0–1	0
INS	2–6	1
INS/FRU	7–11	2
FRU	12+	3+

Comp. % (Lines + Between)	
Errors	%
0	100
1	83
2	66
3	50
4	33
5	17
6	0

M 7. How well do you think you answered these factual and thought questions? Point to the picture that is closest to the way you think you answered.

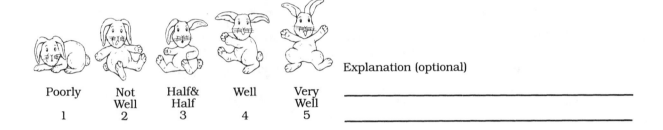

Poorly	Not Well	Half& Half	Well	Very Well
1	2	3	4	5

Explanation (optional)

_____

_____

READING BEYOND THE LINES

Score: **0** for unacceptable, **1** for acceptable

Score

SC 8. Is there any danger today in flying kites? (*yes, electric lines—that is why we go to large fields*)

_____   _____

PS 9. Would you let little children play with kites in their back yards? (*not without checking for power lines*)

_____   _____

M   10. How well do you think you answered these last two questions? Point to the picture
that is closest to the way you feel.

Poorly	Not Well	Half& Half	Well	Very Well
1	2	3	4	5

Explanation (optional)

_____

_____

OE   11. Do you think that kites would be a good way of sending messages? Why?
Why not? (*not really—for example, you would need for it to be daylight and
you'd need some wind to fly one*)

Score

Oral Response Notes:

_____   _____

_____

Optional: Following initial discussion of question 11, ask the student to
write his or her answer on a separate sheet of paper. Attach this writing
sample to the test materials, and record the student's score here.   _____

GRADE 4 PASSAGE FORM B: TEACHER'S RECORDING FORM

PRIOR KNOWLEDGE

What does a shepherd do? _____

Where do villagers live? _____

What do you think would happen if a wolf met a sheep? _____

Now you are going to listen to (or read) a story about a shepherd boy who got in the habit of telling lies. Then I will ask you some questions about what you have heard and what you thought about it.

The Shepherd Boy and the Wolf	**Notes:**
A shepherd boy was tending his flock near a village and thought it would be great fun to trick the villagers by pretending that a wolf was attacking the sheep. He shouted out, "Wolf! Wolf!" and when the villagers came running up, he laughed at them for being so easily tricked. He tried this hoax more than once. Every time the villagers ran to help the boy, they found that they had been tricked again, and there was no wolf at all.	
At last, a wolf really did come, and the boy cried, "Wolf! Wolf!" as loud as he could, but the people were so used to hearing him cry "Wolf!" that they took no notice of his cries for help. So there was nothing to stop the wolf, and it killed many sheep.	
The moral of this story is: No one believes a liar, even when he tells the truth.	

Reading Time = ___ min. ___ sec. = ___ sec.   Words per Minute = 9,060 ÷ ___ sec. = _____ WPM

EJ How much did you enjoy this story? Point to the picture that is closest to the way you feel.

Show student the "rating card" reproduced here. Briefly review the meaning of each choice, and circle the number of the student's choice. Then on the questions that follow, you may indicate the "value" of responses by recording a "**–**" for responses that are clearly incongruent, or illogical, or a "**+**" for any that are exceptionally full or detailed.

Very Little	Little	Half& Half	Much	Very Much
1	2	3	4	5

Explanation (optional)

_____

_____

READING THE LINES

Score: **0** for incorrect, **1** for correct
Value: **–** for incongruent, **+** for congruent

Score   Value

F 1. What was the shepherd boy's job (*taking care of the sheep*)

_____   _____ _____

F 2. What idea did he think of as a way to have fun? (*tricking the villagers by pretending that a wolf was attacking the sheep*)

_____   _____ _____

F 3. What did the villagers do when the boy first shouted "Wolf!"? (*they came running to help*)

_____   _____ _____

V 4. What does the word "hoax" mean in this passage? (*a trick or a joke*)

_____   _____ _____

READING BETWEEN THE LINES

Score   *Value*

I   5.   Did the villagers think that a wolf might harm the sheep? (*yes—that's why they came running when the boy called*)

_____   _____   _____

I   6.   Why didn't the villagers come when the wolf was really killing the sheep? (*they didn't believe the boy when he finally told the truth*)

_____   _____   _____

Scoring Guide—The Shepherd Boy and the Wolf		
Level	Word Recognition Errors	Comprehension Errors (Questions 1–6)
IND	0–2	0
INS	3–8	1
INS/FRU	9–15	2
FRU	16+	3+

Comp. % (Lines + Between)	
Errors	%
0	100
1	83
2	66
3	50
4	33
5	17
6	0

M   7.   How well do you think you answered these factual and thought questions? Point to the picture that is closest to the way you think you answered.

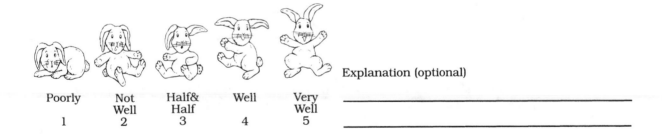

Poorly	Not Well	Half& Half	Well	Very Well
1	2	3	4	5

Explanation (optional)

_____

_____

READING BEYOND THE LINES

Score: **0** for unacceptable, **1** for acceptable

CE   8.   Tell how much you agree with this statement: *"Trust is more important than fun."* Point to the picture that shows the way you feel. (*The student's explanation should indicate that fun is important, but trust is more so, and that it is possible to have fun without destroying trust.*)

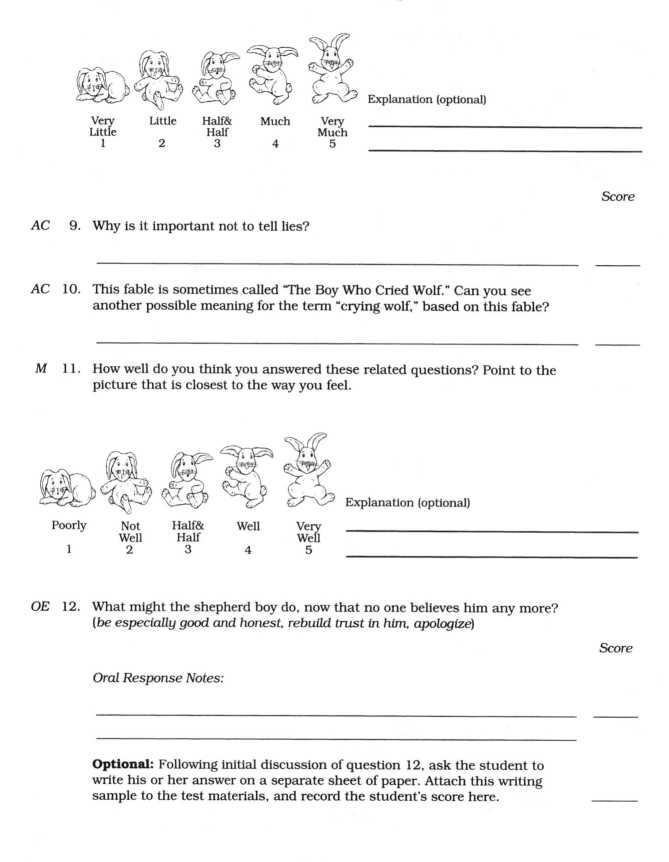

Very Little 1   Little 2   Half & Half 3   Much 4   Very Much 5

Explanation (optional)

_____

_____

Score

AC   9.   Why is it important not to tell lies?

_____   _____

AC   10.   This fable is sometimes called "The Boy Who Cried Wolf." Can you see another possible meaning for the term "crying wolf," based on this fable?

_____   _____

M   11.   How well do you think you answered these related questions? Point to the picture that is closest to the way you feel.

Poorly 1   Not Well 2   Half & Half 3   Well 4   Very Well 5

Explanation (optional)

_____

_____

OE   12.   What might the shepherd boy do, now that no one believes him any more? (*be especially good and honest, rebuild trust in him, apologize*)

Score

Oral Response Notes:

_____   _____

_____

Optional: Following initial discussion of question 12, ask the student to write his or her answer on a separate sheet of paper. Attach this writing sample to the test materials, and record the student's score here.   _____

GRADE 5 PASSAGE FORM B: TEACHER'S RECORDING FORM

PRIOR KNOWLEDGE

Can you tell me some ways that people sent messages before we had telephones and radios?

_____

What does it mean to communicate? _____

What is a signal? _____

Now you are going to listen to (or read) a passage about how people sent messages long ago. Then I will ask you some questions about what you have heard and what you thought about it.

Signals and Messages	**Notes:**
Even in the earliest times, people tried different ways of communicating quickly. Sometimes they sent letters by messenger. Sometimes they communicated by using signals.	
Greek soldiers sent messages by turning their shields toward the sun. The flashes of reflected light could be seen several miles away. The enemy did not know what the flashes meant. But other Greek soldiers understood what the message said.	
In later years, Roman soldiers built long rows of signal towers. When they had a message, the soldiers shouted it from tower to tower. If there were enough towers and enough soldiers with loud voices, important news could be sent over a long distance.	
American Indians used smoke signals to send messages. In Africa, people learned to send messages by beating on a series of large drums.	

Reading Time = ___ min. ___ sec. = ___ sec.   Words per Minute = 7,920 ÷ ___ sec. = _____ WPM

EJ How much do you think you would enjoy listening to the rest of this passage? Point to the picture that is closest to the way you feel.

> Show student the "rating card" reproduced here. Briefly review the meaning of each choice, and circle the number of the student's choice. Then on the questions that follow, you may indicate the "value" of responses by recording a "−" for responses that are clearly incongruent, or illogical, or a "+" for any that are exceptionally full or detailed.

Very Little	Little	Half& Half	Much	Very Much
1	2	3	4	5

Explanation (optional)

_____

_____

READING THE LINES

> Score: **0** for incorrect, **1** for correct
> Value: **−** for incongruent, **+** for congruent

Score   Value

F 1. According to the first paragraph, what was one of the two basic ways of sending messages long ago? (*by messengers or by signals*)

_____   ____   ____

F 2. How did Greek soldiers send their messages? (*by turning their shields toward the sun*)

_____   ____   ____

F 3. How did Roman soldiers sometimes send their messages? (*by shouting from one signal tower to another*)

_____   ____   ____

F 4. How did African people send messages? (*by beating on drums*)

_____   ____   ____

V 5. What does the word "communicate" mean in this passage? (*to send and receive messages*)

_____   ____   ____

READING BETWEEN THE LINES

Score   *Value*

I   6.   Why would Greek soldiers have a problem sending their shield messages at night? (*they needed sunlight to reflect off their shields*)

_____   ____   ____

I   7.   Were the towers used by the Romans placed close together or far apart? (*they were far enough apart that people had to shout to be heard*)

_____   ____   ____

Scoring Guide—Signals and Messages		
Level	Word Recognition Errors	Comprehension Errors (Questions 1–7)
IND	0–1	0–1
INS	2–7	2
INS/FRU	8–13	3
FRU	14+	4+

Comp. % (Lines + Between)	
Errors	%
0	100
1	86
2	71
3	57
4	43
5	29
6	14
7	0

M   8.   How well do you think you answered these questions? Point to the picture that is closest to the way you think you answered.

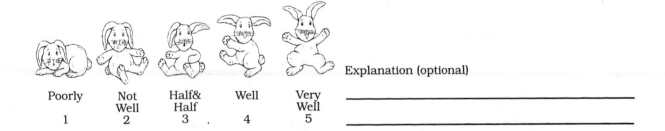

Poorly	Not Well	Half& Half	Well	Very Well
1	2	3 .	4	5

Explanation (optional)

_____

_____

READING BEYOND THE LINES

> *Score:* **0** for unacceptable, **1** for acceptable

Score

SC   9.   Why didn't early people just send written messages? (*sometimes this was too slow; or, many people could not read*)

_____   ____

SC   10.   What *discovery* made it possible to invent modern communication devices like radios, record players, televisions, and so on? (*electricity*)

_____   _____

PS   11.   How would you send a message for help today if you were lost on a deserted island?

_____   _____

SC   12.   Name four modern means of communicating across distance.

_____   _____

M   13.   How well do you think you answered these related questions? Point to the picture that is closest to the way you feel.

Poorly	Not Well	Half& Half	Well	Very Well
1	2	3	4	5

Explanation (optional)

_____

_____

OE   14.   At sea, ships can use different flags or flashing lights to communicate messages. When might this be a useful means of communication for sailors to know about today? (*for occasions when they must keep the radio silent or their radio may be broken*)

Score

Oral Response Notes:

_____   _____

_____

Optional: Following initial discussion of question 14, ask the student to write his or her answer on a separate sheet of paper. Attach this writing sample to the test materials, and record the student's score here.   _____

GRADE 6 PASSAGE FORM B: TEACHER'S RECORDING FORM

PRIOR KNOWLEDGE

Have you ever been fooled by someone? Tell me a little about it. _____

What does it mean to sue someone? _____

What does the word "cure" mean? _____

You are going to listen to (or read) a story about a doctor who tried to fool his patient. Then I will ask you some questions about what you have heard and what you thought about it.

The Old Woman and the Doctor

An old woman became almost totally blind from a disease of the eyes and, after consulting a doctor, made an agreement with him in the presence of witnesses. She would pay him a high fee if he cured her, while if he failed he was to receive nothing. The doctor accordingly prescribed a course of treatment, and every time he paid her a visit, he took away with him some article out of the house. When he visited her for the last time and when the cure was complete and the woman could see, there was nothing left.

When the old woman saw that the house was empty, she refused to pay him his fee, and, after repeated refusals on her part, he sued her before the magistrates for payment of her debt. On being brought into court, she was ready with her defense.

"The doctor," said she, "has stated the facts about our agreement correctly. I agreed to pay him a fee if he cured me, and he, on his part, promised to charge nothing if he failed. Now, he says I am cured, but I say that I am blinder than ever, and I can prove what I say. When my eyes were bad, I could still see well enough to know that my house contained a certain amount of furniture and other things. But now, while according to him I am cured, I am entirely unable to see anything at all."

Notes:

Reading Time = ___ min. ___ sec. = ___ sec.   Words per Minute = 14,580 ÷ ___ sec. = _____ WPM

EJ   How much did you enjoy this story? Point to the picture that is closest to the way you feel.

> Show student the "rating card" reproduced here. Briefly review the meaning of each choice, and circle the number of the student's choice. Then on the questions that follow, you may indicate the "value" of responses by recording a "−" for responses that are clearly incongruent, or illogical, or a "+" for any that are exceptionally full or detailed.

Very Little 1	Little 2	Half& Half 3	Much 4	Very Much 5

Explanation (optional)

_____

_____

READING THE LINES

> *Score:* **0** for incorrect, **1** for correct
> *Value:* **−** for incongruent, **+** for congruent

                                                                    Score   *Value*

F   1. How did the old woman become almost blind? (*from a disease of the eyes*)

_____   ____   ____

F   2. What was the agreement between the old woman and the doctor? (*if the doctor cured her, she would pay him a high fee, but if he failed, he was to receive nothing*)

_____   ____   ____

F   3. What did the doctor do when he visited her each time? (*each time, he took something from her house away with him*)

_____   ____   ____

F   4. What did the old woman do when the doctor gave her the bill for curing her blindness? (*she refused to pay several times*)

_____   ____   ____

V   5.   What does the word "consulting" mean in the phrase: ". . .after consulting a doctor"? (*asking for advice from an expert*)

_____   _____   _____

V   6.   What is a "magistrate"? (*a judge*)

_____   _____   _____

READING BETWEEN THE LINES

                                          Score   Value

I   7.   Was the old woman cured of her blindness by the end of the story? How do you know? (*yes—because she could see that nothing was in her house*)

_____   _____   _____

I   8.   Did the doctor think at first that he could cure the old woman? Give reasons to prove your answer. (*probably not—every time he visited the old woman, he took something from her house, thinking that she would never see anyway*)

_____   _____   _____

I   9.   How do you think the court ruled in this case—in favor of the doctor or of the old woman? Why? (*in favor of the old woman: the doctor had deceived her, and it was not even certain that he was responsible for her cure*)

_____   _____   _____

Scoring Guide—The Old Woman and the Doctor		
Level	Word Recognition Errors	Comprehension Errors (Questions 1–9)
IND	0–3	0–1
INS	4–12	2
INS/FRU	13–24	3–4
FRU	25+	5+

Comp. % (Lines + Between)	
Errors	%
0	100
1	89
2	78
3	67
4	56
5	45
6	33
7	22
8	11
9	0

M   10.   How well do you think you answered these questions? Point to the picture that is closest to the way you think you answered.

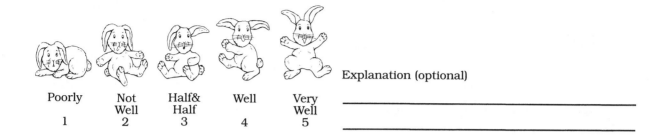

Poorly	Not Well	Half& Half	Well	Very Well
1	2	3	4	5

Explanation (optional)

_____

_____

READING BEYOND THE LINES

> *Score:* **0** for unacceptable, **1** for acceptable

Score

CE   11.   Who was wiser, the old woman or the doctor? Why? (*the old woman—she tricked the doctor with his own claim*)

_____   _____

SC   12.   Do you think there are doctors in the real world who deceive their patients for money? (*yes, every group is likely to contain some who are deceptive*)

_____   _____

PS   13.   What would you do if you were deceived by someone? (*it depends on who did it and for how much*)

_____   _____

EX   14.   How did the old woman prove that the doctor did not deserve a high fee? (*by telling that her things were gone, and therefore the doctor was a thief*)

_____   _____

M   15.   How well do you think you answered these related questions? Point to the picture that is closest to the way you think you answered.

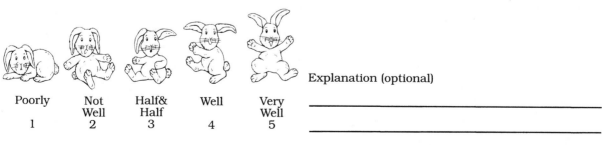

Poorly	Not Well	Half& Half	Well	Very Well
1	2	3	4	5

Explanation (optional)

_____

_____

OE 16. Explain why you think each of these would be a good or poor title for this piece:

    A. Blind, But Not Dumb

    B. Only Fools Trust Others

    C. To Be Fooled, One Must Have Trusted

(To evaluate the student's response, look for evidence that the student's thinking becomes less emotional and more reflective while reprocessing the story facts and relating life experiences. Here are some sample points students might mention:

    A. *This title has the best literary merit, but the woman was not "blind"—only partially sighted.*

    B. *This title is a poor choice because it suggests that all who trust are fools, and it would be intolerable to live without some trust.*

    C. *This title is good and carries the point, but it is a bit too "teachy" to be entertaining.)*

                                                        Score

Oral Response Notes:

_____   _____

_____

Optional: Following initial discussion of question 16, ask the student to write his or her answer on a separate sheet of paper. Attach this writing sample to the test materials, and record the student's score here.   _____

GRADE 7 PASSAGE FORM B: TEACHER'S RECORDING FORM

PRIOR KNOWLEDGE

Have you ever heard any of the legends that people of long ago created to explain things like the sun's movement across the sky? Can you give me an example? _____

What does it mean to envy someone? _____

What is a temple? _____

You are going to listen to (or read) the beginning of a legend that is about the creation of the Sun and the Moon. Then I will ask you some questions about what you have heard and what you thought about it.

The Creation of the Sun and the Moon

Notes:

A legend among the Indians of Mexico tells how once when the world was young, the Sun brought joy to people, how the Sun then was destroyed by evil, and how a singularly brave young Indian undertook a perilous journey to create a new Sun. This is how the legend begins.

Once people lived in peace on Earth and in true happiness. The golden Sun gave them light and warmth, enriched their fields with corn, painted the flowers in radiant colors, filled the trees with sweet fruit in abundance, and caused the birds to sing.

Thus, it was only natural for people to revere the Sun as the source of all blessings and richness and happiness on Earth. To thank the Good Gods for the Sun, people built great temples and pyramids of stone and sang beautiful songs of praise.

But the Gods of Evil and Darkness envied the happiness that people enjoyed on Earth. So it came to pass that these gods left the deep ravines where they lived and their homes on the shores of subterranean lakes and rivers and went forth to do battle with the Good Gods so they might destroy them and rule the world.

Reading Time = ___ min. ___ sec. = ___ sec.   Words per Minute = 12,240 ÷ ___ sec. = _____ WPM

EJ   How much do you think you would enjoy listening to the rest of this legend? Point to the picture that is closest to the way you feel.

> Show student the "rating card" reproduced here. Briefly review the meaning of each choice, and circle the number of the student's choice. Then on the questions that follow, you may indicate the "value" of responses by recording a "−" for responses that are clearly incongruent, or illogical, or a "**+**" for any that are exceptionally full or detailed.

Very Little	Little	Half& Half	Much	Very Much
1	2	3	4	5

Explanation (optional)

_____

_____

READING THE LINES

> *Score:* **0** for incorrect, **1** for correct
> *Value:* **−** for incongruent, **+** for congruent

                                                                    Score   *Value*

F   1. Where is this legend from? (*Mexico*)

_____   _____   _____

F   2. According to the legend, how did people live when the sun gave them light and warmth? (*in peace and happiness*)

_____   _____   _____

F   3. What did they do to show their thanks to the Sun? (*they built temples and pyramids and sang songs of praise*)

_____   _____   _____

F   4. Why did the Gods of Evil launch a battle against the Good Gods? (*they didn't want people to be happy; or, they envied the Good Gods; or, they wanted to rule the world*)

_____   _____   _____

V   5. What does the word "singularly" mean in this sentence: ". . . and how a singularly brave young Indian undertook a perilous journey to create a new Sun"? (*unusually/ particularly / especially*)

_____   _____   _____

READING BETWEEN THE LINES

Score   *Value*

I   6. Do you think that these people believed in only one god? (*no—they refer to good and evil gods*)

———————————————————   ——   ——

I   7. What do you suppose the next part of the legend will be about? (*how the gods of evil attempted to destroy the sun*)

———————————————————   ——   ——

Scoring Guide—The Creation of the Sun and the Moon		
Level	Word Recognition Errors	Comprehension Errors (Questions 1–7)
IND	0–2	0–1
INS	3–10	2
INS/FRU	11–20	3
FRU	21+	4+

Comp. % (Lines + Between)	
Errors	%
0	100
1	86
2	71
3	57
4	43
5	29
6	14
7	0

M   8. How well do you think you answered these questions? Point to the picture that is closest to the way you think you answered.

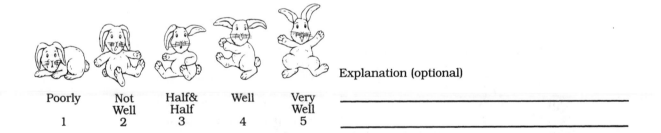

Poorly	Not Well	Half& Half	Well	Very Well
1	2	3	4	5

Explanation (optional)

———————————————————

———————————————————

READING BEYOND THE LINES

Score: **0** for unacceptable, **1** for acceptable

Score

SC   9. It has been said that, one way or another, the sun is the source of all living things. What do you think of this? (*it sounds probable, but there may be exceptions that I don't know about*)

———————————————————   ——

SC 10. Are there any buildings that can be found in our towns and cities that are similar in their purpose to the pyramids built by these primitive peoples? (*yes—churches, temples, synagogues, and other places of worship*)

_____   _____

CE 11. The Evil Gods felt envy and that led them to try to do harm. Is there a difference between envy and admiration? Explain. (*admiration is positive and often leads to greater effort to achieve the levels of those who are admired*)

_____   _____

M 12. How well do you think you answered these last few questions? Point to the picture that is closest to the way you feel.

Poorly	Not Well	Half & Half	Well	Very Well	Explanation (optional)
1	2	3	4	5	

_____

_____

OE 13. Why do you suppose so many different early peoples believed in "good gods" and "bad gods"? (*to explain the good and bad things that happen in life*)

Score

Oral Response Notes:

_____   _____

_____

Optional: Following initial discussion of question 13, ask the student to write his or her answer on a separate sheet of paper. Attach this writing sample to the test materials, and record the student's score here.   _____

GRADE 8 PASSAGE FORM B: TEACHER'S RECORDING FORM

PRIOR KNOWLEDGE

Of the birds you know, which is the prettiest? _____

What is a plume? _____

Who was Jupiter? _____

Now you are going to listen to (or read) a fable about a jackdaw. Many people think that the jackdaw is a really ugly bird. Then I will ask you some questions about the fable and what you thought about it.

The Vain Jackdaw

Notes:

Jupiter announced that he intended to appoint a king over the birds and named a day on which they were to appear before his throne, when he would select the most beautiful of them all to be their ruler. Wishing to look their best for the occasion, the birds went to the banks of a stream, where they busied themselves in washing and preening their feathers.

The jackdaw was there along with the rest and realized that, with his ugly plumage, he would have no chance of being chosen as he was. So he waited until they were all gone, then picked up the most colorful of the feathers they had dropped and fastened them about his own body, with the result that he looked grander than any of them.

When the appointed day came, the birds assembled before Jupiter's throne. After passing them in review, he was about to make the jackdaw king when all the rest set upon the appointed king, stripped him of his borrowed plumes, and exposed him for the jackdaw that he was.

Reading Time = ___ min. ___ sec. = ___ sec.   Words per Minute = 10,680 ÷ ___ sec. = _____ WPM

EJ   How much did you enjoy this fable? Point to the picture that is closest to the way you feel.

Show student the "rating card" reproduced here. Briefly review the meaning of each choice, and circle the number of the student's choice. Then on the questions that follow, you may indicate the "value" of responses by recording a "–" for responses that are clearly incongruent, or illogical, or a "+" for any that are exceptionally full or detailed.

Very Little	Little	Half& Half	Much	Very Much
1	2	3	4	5

Explanation (optional)

_____

_____

READING THE LINES

Score: **0** for incorrect, **1** for correct
Value: **–** for incongruent, **+** for congruent

Score   *Value*

F   1. What did Jupiter intend to do in this story? (*appoint a king over the birds*)

_____   ____   ____

F   2. What was the requirement Jupiter set for the king of the birds? (*he must be the most beautiful of them all*)

_____   ____   ____

F   3. What was the birds' reaction to Jupiter's announcement? (*they began to wash and straighten their feathers*)

_____   ____   ____

F   4. How did the Jackdaw decide that he would compete with the more beautiful birds? (*he picked up their most colorful feathers and fastened them about his own body*)

_____   ____   ____

V   5. What do you suppose the word "preen" means in this passage? (*to adjust the feathers*)

_____   ____   ____

V 6. What do you suppose the expression means that the birds "set upon the appointed king"? (*they attacked him*)

_____   ____   ____

READING BETWEEN THE LINES

Score   *Value*

I 7. How do you suppose the other birds knew that the jackdaw was in disguise? (*they had never seen one bird with so many different colors; or, they may have recognized their own feathers*)

_____   ____   ____

I 8. Do you think the jackdaw expected that the other birds would know what he had done? Give reasons to support your answer. (*no—if he had expected this, he probably wouldn't have disguised himself*)

_____   ____   ____

Scoring Guide—The Vain Jackdaw		
Level	Word Recognition Errors	Comprehension Errors (Questions 1–8)
IND	0–2	0–1
INS	3–9	2
INS/FRU	10–17	3–4
FRU	18+	5+

Comp. % (Lines + Between)	
Errors	%
0	100
1	88
2	75
3	63
4	50
5	38
6	25
7	13
8	0

M 9. How well do you think you answered these questions? Point to the picture that is closest to the way you think you answered.

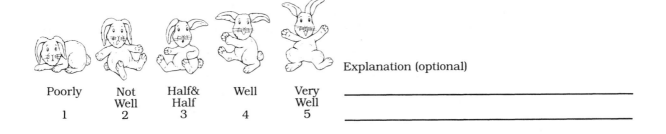

Poorly	Not Well	Half& Half	Well	Very Well
1	2	3	4	5

Explanation (optional)

_____

_____

READING BEYOND THE LINES

> *Score:* **0** for unacceptable, **1** for acceptable

Score

CE 10. Do you think the jackdaw was wiser than the other birds? Why or why not? (*it is not wise to pretend to be something that you are not*)

_____   _____

SC 11. Which of these birds would you make a king of birds: the eagle, the peacock, or the owl? Explain your answer. (*answers will vary according to what student values most*)

_____   _____

CE 12. Do people ever try to cover up or change their looks? (*yes—we do it all the time with cosmetics, hairdos, clothes, etc.*)

_____   _____

M 13. How well do you think you answered these related questions? Point to the picture that is closest to the way you feel.

Poorly	Not Well	Half& Half	Well	Very Well
1	2	3	4	5

Explanation (optional)

_____

_____

OE 14. Was Jupiter wise to make beauty the only requirement for being a king of birds? Why?

Score

Oral Response Notes:

_____   _____

_____

Optional: Following initial discussion of question 14, ask the student to write his or her answer on a separate sheet of paper. Attach this writing sample to the test materials, and record the student's score here.   _____

GRADE 9 PASSAGE FORM B: TEACHER'S RECORDING FORM

PRIOR KNOWLEDGE

Why do people dress in special ways to go to different kinds of events and activities?

_____

What is an emperor?_____

What sort of people would be in a king's court? _____

Now you are going to listen to (or read) part of a selection about people at a wrestling match. Then I will ask you some questions about what you have heard and what you thought about it.

Awaiting the Match

All the ladies and gentlemen of the court were waiting in a special courtyard for the wrestling to begin. They wore many robes, one on top of another, heavy with embroidery and gold cloth, and sweat ran down their faces and froze in the winter afternoon. The gentlemen had long swords so weighted with gold and precious stones that they could never have used them, even if they had known how. The court ladies, their long black hair hanging down behind, had their faces painted dead white, which made them look frightened. They had pulled out their real eyebrows and painted new ones high above the place where eyebrows are supposed to be, and this made them all look as though they were very surprised at something.

Behind a screen sat the Emperor—by himself, because he was too noble for ordinary people to look at. He was a lonely old man with a kind, tired face. He hoped the wrestling would end quickly so he could go to his room and write poems.

Notes:

_Reading Time = ___ min. ___ sec. = ___ sec.   Words per Minute = 10,440 ÷ ___ sec. = _____ WPM_

EJ   How much do you think you would enjoy listening to the rest of this selection? Point to the picture that is closest to the way you feel.

Show student the "rating card" reproduced here. Briefly review the meaning of each choice, and circle the number of the student's choice. Then on the questions that follow, you may indicate the "value" of responses by recording a "–" for responses that are clearly incongruent, or illogical, or a "+" for any that are exceptionally full or detailed.

Very Little	Little	Half& Half	Much	Very Much
1	2	3	4	5

Explanation (optional)

_____

_____

READING THE LINES

Score: **0** for incorrect, **1** for correct
Value: **–** for incongruent, **+** for congruent

                                                                    Score   *Value*

F   1.   What were the people doing at the beginning of this selection?
           (*they were waiting for the wrestling to begin*)

           _____   _____   _____

F   2.   What was unusual about their clothes? (*they wore many robes, one
           on top of another, heavy with embroidery and gold cloth*)

           _____   _____   _____

F   3.   How did the court ladies paint their faces and eyebrows? (*they
           painted their faces dead white, plucked their eyebrows, and painted
           new eyebrows high above the place where they are supposed to be*)

           _____   _____   _____

F   4.   Why did the Emperor sit behind the screen? (*he was too noble for
           ordinary people to look at*)

           _____   _____   _____

Score   Value

V   5. What does the word "embroidery" mean in this story? (*a special kind of sewing used as decoration*)

_____   _____ _____

READING BETWEEN THE LINES

I   6. Why did the gentlemen bring their long swords? (*for decoration; or, to show their place in society; or, because it was the custom*)

_____   _____ _____

I   7. Do you think that the Emperor enjoyed wrestling? Explain your answer. (*no—he hoped it would end soon so that he could go to his room and write poems*)

_____   _____ _____

I   8. What do you suppose the remainder of this story will be about? (*about the wrestling match*)

_____   _____ _____

Scoring Guide—Awaiting the Match		
Level	Word Recognition Errors	Comprehension Errors (Questions 1–8)
IND	0–2	0–1
INS	3–8	2
INS/FRU	9–17	3–4
FRU	18+	5+

Comp. % (Lines + Between)	
Errors	%
0	100
1	88
2	75
3	63
4	50
5	38
6	25
7	13
8	0

M   9. How well do you think you answered these questions? Point to the picture that is closest to the way you think you answered.

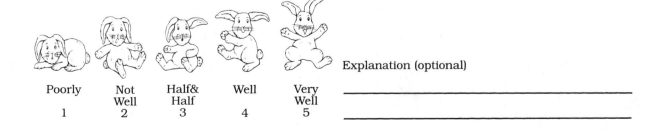

Poorly	Not Well	Half& Half	Well	Very Well
1	2	3	4	5

Explanation (optional)

_____

_____

READING BEYOND THE LINES

> *Score:* **0** for unacceptable, **1** for acceptable

Score

SC 10. In what country do you suppose this story might take place? (*Japan, China, or other Asian land*)

_____ _____

CE 11. According to the second paragraph, do you think that the Emperor had a happy life? Explain your answer. (*no, he was a lonely old man*)

_____ _____

M 12. How well do you think you answered these related questions? Point to the picture that is closest to the way you feel.

Poorly	Not Well	Half& Half	Well	Very Well
1	2	3	4	5

Explanation (optional)

_____

_____

OE 13. Obviously it is not a good idea to have an emperor with absolute power and who is treated like a god. But, how do you feel about the idea of having a king or a queen with *limited* power, the way they do in Jordan or Saudi Arabia? (*there is nothing basically wrong with it, but the people have less voice in how they will be governed*)

Score

Oral Response Notes:

_____ _____

_____

Optional: Following initial discussion of question 13, ask the student to write his or her answer on a separate sheet of paper. Attach this writing sample to the test materials, and record the student's score here. _____

PART 3

STUDENT BOOKLET
Word Lists

WORD CARD A

1. be	1. car
2. play	2. new
3. a	3. not
4. you	4. with
5. can	5. help
6. he	6. her
7. look	7. up
8. run	8. come
9. said	9. work
10. here	10. this
11. but	11. some
12. did	12. now
13. the	13. took
14. big	14. been
15. man	15. take

WORD CARD B

1. are	1. our
2. is	2. way
3. by	3. town
4. when	4. send
5. jump	5. wide
6. how	6. young
7. night	7. early
8. today	8. believe
9. would	9. straight
10. thank	10. people
11. which	11. between
12. spring	12. thought
13. something	13. already
14. where	14. children
15. school	15. point

WORD CARD C

1. city	1. decided	1. cruel
2. moment	2. wrecked	2. kerosene
3. middle	3. served	3. business
4. frightened	4. pint	4. melted
5. different	5. amazed	5. develop
6. move	6. silent	6. abolish
7. several	7. letter	7. considered
8. exclaimed	8. study	8. especially
9. drew	9. realized	9. discussed
10. since	10. improved	10. furious
11. ground	11. flattered	11. stirred
12. enough	12. entered	12. splendid
13. brought	13. beauty	13. acquainted
14. though	14. coffin	14. grim
15. rough	15. Mrs.	15. ignore

WORD CARD D

1. bridge	1. amber	1. universal
2. luxurious	2. nuclear	2. legislator
3. commercial	3. dominion	3. limitation
4. remained	4. manual	4. pretext
5. hysterical	5. sundry	5. persuasive
6. apparatus	6. reformatory	6. intrigue
7. ventured	7. capillary	7. flourish
8. generation	8. parson	8. pavilion
9. comment	9. blight	9. immaculate
10. biographer	10. mockery	10. acquired
11. necessity	11. wrestle	11. lyric
12. society	12. mission	12. entrust
13. caravan	13. satisfy	13. navigator
14. relativity	14. scripture	14. terrified
15. dainty	15. century	15. reputation

WORD CARD E

1. fascinating	1. persistent	1. galore
2. conscientious	2. adorn	2. abdicate
3. isolation	3. strenuous	3. rotunda
4. adolescence	4. baroness	4. cahoots
5. descendants	5. nausea	5. capitalism
6. molecule	6. desegregate	6. cantankerous
7. emissary	7. limerick	7. prevaricate
8. ritual	8. linguist	8. debutante
9. fotification	9. lore	9. effigy
10. momentous	10. aspen	10. exonerate
11. illuminate	11. lynch	11. gaudy
12. vulnerable	12. amnesty	12. cantilever
13. moccasins	13. malcontent	13. piebald
14. kinship	14. barometer	14. dastard
15. hideous	15. carnivorous	15. crunch

Form A Passages

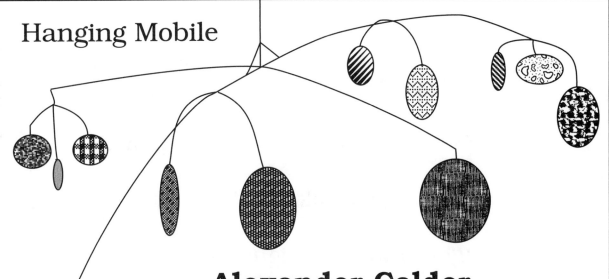

Hanging Mobile

Alexander Calder

Alexander Calder was a great artist. He started making things when he was five.

Alexander's mother and father were artists, too. They were happy that their son liked to make things.

Many people know and love Alexander Calder's art today. He is best known for making mobiles, a new kind of hanging art.

The Crab and His Mother

An Old Crab said to her son, "Why do you walk sideways like that, my son? You ought to walk straight." The Young Crab replied, "Show me how, dear mother, and I'll follow your example." The Old Crab tried and tried, but then she saw how foolish she had been to find fault with her child.

The Desert: What Lives There

The desert is a place that gets very little rainfall. The ground is often sandy and rocky. When the sun beats down, the sand and rocks grow hot and dry. It is hard to imagine that a place like this is full of living things.

All living things need food, water, and some kind of shelter to survive. Some plants and animals are well suited to survive in the desert. They can live off the food, water, and shelter that are there.

The cactus is one kind of plant that is suited to survive in the desert. The cactus has a special way of getting water in the dry desert soil. It spreads its roots out close to the top of the ground. When rain comes, the cactus roots soak up the water quickly before it drains deep into the sand.

Once a cactus plant gets water, it can store it for the dry days ahead. A cactus can store enough water from one rainstorm to last a long time.

The Fox and the Crow

A Crow was sitting on a branch of a tree with a piece of cheese in her beak when a Fox observed her and set his brain to work to discover some way of getting the cheese. Coming and standing under the tree, he looked up and said, "What a noble bird I see above me! Her beauty is without equal; the hue of her plumage is rare. If only her voice were as sweet as her looks are lovely, she surely should be Queen of the Birds." The Crow was very flattered by this, and just to show the Fox that she could sing, she gave a loud caw. Down came the cheese, of course, and the Fox, snatching it up, said, "You have a voice, madam, but what you don't have are brains."

The Big Wave

Kino lived on a farm. The farm lay on the side of a mountain in Japan. The fields were terraced by walls of stone, each one of them like a broad step up the mountain.

Above all the fields stood the farmhouse that was Kino's home. Sometimes he felt the climb was a hard one, especially when he had been working in the lowest field and he wanted his supper. But after he had eaten each night and each morning, he was glad that he lived so high up, because he could look down on the broad blue ocean at the foot of the mountain.

The mountain rose so steeply out of the ocean that there was only a strip of sandy shore at its foot. Upon this strip was the small fishing village where Kino's good friend Jiya lived.

On days when the sky was bright and the winds mild, the ocean lay so calm and blue that it was hard to believe that it could ever be cruel and angry. Yet even Kino never quite forgot that when he dived down under the warm blue surface, the water was cold and green. When the sun shone, the deep water was still. But when the deep water moved and heaved and stirred, ah, then Kino was glad that his father was a farmer and not a fisherman.

And yet, one day, it was the earth that brought the big wave. Deep under the ocean, fires raged in the heart of the earth. The icy cold of the water could not chill those fires. Rocks were melted and boiled, but they could not break through the crust of the ocean's bed. At last the steam grew so strong that it forced its way through to the mouth of the far-off volcano.

The Frogs Who Wanted a King

Time was when the Frogs were discontented because they had no one to rule over them. So the Frogs sent a representative to Jupiter to ask him to give them a king.

Jupiter, despising the folly of their request, cast a log into the pool where they lived. He said, "Here, this log will be your king." The Frogs were terrified at first by the splash and scuttled away into the deepest parts of the pool; but by and by, when they saw that the log remained motionless, one by one they ventured to the surface again, and before long, growing bolder, they began to feel such contempt for it that they even took to sitting upon it. Thinking that a king of that sort was an insult to their dignity, they sent another message to Jupiter, begging him to take away the sluggish king he had given them and to give them a better one. Jupiter, annoyed at being pestered in this way, sent a stork to rule over them, who no sooner than he arrived among them began to catch and eat the Frogs as fast as he could.

Whaling

Before the discovery of oil in the ground, oil from whales was used to lubricate the wheels of machinery and to fuel lamps. Whalebone was used in the nineteenth century for a number of practical and decorative household items. It was also an important part of women's wardrobes in the days when corsets and hoop skirts were worn.

As more and more ships hunted whales to satisfy a growing market for whale oil and bone, trips grew longer and longer. Rather than spend a morning rowing a boat from the beach, nineteenth-century whalers took ships around the world on hunts that lasted for years. Trips three to five years long were common. Once home, a whaling man stopped barely long enough to see his children before he was off to sea again. The risks of whaling were such that the odds were two to one against any sailors returning from such a trip.

The Cobbler Turned Doctor

A very unskillful cobbler, finding himself unable to make a living at his trade, gave up mending boots and took to doctoring instead. He let it be known that he had the secret of a universal antidote against all poisons, and he acquired no small reputation, thanks to his talent for promoting himself. One day, however, the cobbler-turned-doctor fell very ill, and the king of the country decided he would test the value of his remedy. Calling, therefore, for a cup, he poured out a dose of the antidote and, pretending to mix poison with it, really added a little water and commanded him to drink it. Terrified by the fear of being poisoned, the cobbler confessed that he knew nothing about medicine and that his antidote was worthless. Then the king summoned his subjects and addressed them as follows: "What folly could be greater than yours? Here is this cobbler to whom no one will send his boots to be mended, and yet you have not hesitated to entrust him with your lives!"

James Houston:

Tales of the Far North

Storytelling is an ancient art that all peoples have used to pass on information and to keep the traditions of their society alive. Canadian-born James Houston is a modern-day master storyteller. He skillfully combines his own fascinating stories of adventure with tales of the northern Canadian Indians and Eskimos. These tales have never before been written down.

When James Houston was very young, his father visited the American Indians of the prairies and the Far West almost every year and brought back gifts of beaded moosehide moccasins. Both Houston and his sister watched and listened as their father drew pictures and told them of the wonderful things he had seen.

The family spent many summers on Lake Simcoe in Ontario. There Houston met an old man who introduced the boy to his Ojibwa people. Sometimes the Ojibwa Indians would invite James to fish with them or to gather wild rice from their canoes. They lived in complete harmony with nature. The Ojibwa were not only a strong link with the past but also a strong influence on Houston's future.

Form B Passages

A Better Way

Long ago, many American Indians lived near water. They wanted to travel on the water. They wanted to travel fast. They also wanted to carry things with them when they traveled.

The American Indians found a way to carry their things quickly over the water. They made a new kind of boat called a canoe.

The Fox and the Lion

One day, a fox met a lion. The fox had never seen a lion before. The fox was terrified by the lion's large size and big mouth. He was ready to die with fear.

After a time he met the lion again and was still frightened, but not so much as he had been when he first met the lion.

When he saw the lion for the third time, he was far from being afraid. He went up and began to talk to the lion as if he had known the lion all his life.

Kites in Flight

Did you know that people began flying kites more than two thousand years ago? The Chinese were the first people to invent and use kites. The kites they made were very beautiful. Some were shaped like fish, while others were made to look like dragons.

Sometimes the Chinese people flew kites just for fun. At other times they used kites to help them with their work. They tied a fishing line to the end of a kite. When a fish bit the bait, the kite moved. Then the kite and the fish were pulled in. Chinese farmers put kites in their fields to scare away birds that tried to eat their crops.

The Shepherd Boy and the Wolf

A shepherd boy was tending his flock near a village and thought it would be great fun to trick the villagers by pretending that a wolf was attacking the sheep. He shouted out, "Wolf! Wolf!" and when the villagers came running up, he laughed at them for being so easily tricked. He tried this hoax more than once. Every time the villagers ran to help the boy, they found that they had been tricked again, and there was no wolf at all.

At last, a wolf really did come, and the boy cried, "Wolf! Wolf!" as loud as he could, but the people were so used to hearing him cry "Wolf!" that they took no notice of his cries for help. So there was nothing to stop the wolf, and it killed many sheep.

The moral of this story is: No one believes a liar, even when he tells the truth.

Signals and Messages

Even in the earliest times, people tried different ways of communicating quickly. Sometimes they sent letters by messenger. Sometimes they communicated by using signals.

Greek soldiers sent messages by turning their shields toward the sun. The flashes of reflected light could be seen several miles away. The enemy did not know what the flashes meant. But other Greek soldiers understood what the message said.

In later years, Roman soldiers built long rows of signal towers. When they had a message, the soldiers shouted it from tower to tower. If there were enough towers and enough soldiers with loud voices, important news could be sent over a long distance.

American Indians used smoke signals to send messages. In Africa, people learned to send messages by beating on a series of large drums.

The Old Woman and the Doctor

An old woman became almost totally blind from a disease of the eyes and, after consulting a doctor, made an agreement with him in the presence of witnesses. She would pay him a high fee if he cured her, while if he failed he was to receive nothing. The doctor accordingly prescribed a course of treatment, and every time he paid her a visit, he took away with him some article out of the house. When he visited her for the last time and when the cure was complete and the woman could see, there was nothing left.

When the old woman saw that the house was empty, she refused to pay him his fee, and, after repeated refusals on her part, he sued her before the magistrates for payment of her debt. On being brought into court, she was ready with her defense.

"The doctor," said she, "has stated the facts about our agreement correctly. I agreed to pay him a fee if he cured me, and he, on his part, promised to charge nothing if he failed. Now, he says I am cured, but I say that I am blinder than ever, and I can prove what I say. When my eyes were bad, I could still see well enough to know that my house contained a certain amount of furniture and other things. But now, while according to him I am cured, I am entirely unable to see anything at all."

The Creation of the Sun and the Moon

A legend among the Indians of Mexico tells how once when the world was young, the Sun brought joy to people, how the Sun then was destroyed by evil, and how a singularly brave young Indian undertook a perilous journey to create a new Sun. This is how the legend begins.

Once people lived in peace on Earth and in true happiness. The golden Sun gave them light and warmth, enriched their fields with corn, painted the flowers in radiant colors, filled the trees with sweet fruit in abundance, and caused the birds to sing.

Thus, it was only natural for people to revere the Sun as the source of all blessings and richness and happiness on Earth. To thank the Good Gods for the Sun, people built great temples and pyramids of stone and sang beautiful songs of praise.

But the Gods of Evil and Darkness envied the happiness that people enjoyed on Earth. So it came to pass that these gods left the deep ravines where they lived and their homes on the shores of subterranean lakes and rivers and went forth to do battle with the Good Gods so they might destroy them and rule the world.

The Vain Jackdaw

Jupiter announced that he intended to appoint a king over the birds and named a day on which they were to appear before his throne, when he would select the most beautiful of them all to be their ruler. Wishing to look their best for the occasion, the birds went to the banks of a stream, where they busied themselves in washing and preening their feathers.

The jackdaw was there along with the rest and realized that, with his ugly plumage, he would have no chance of being chosen as he was. So he waited until they were all gone, then picked up the most colorful of the feathers they had dropped and fastened them about his own body, with the result that he looked grander than any of them.

When the appointed day came, the birds assembled before Jupiter's throne. After passing them in review, he was about to make the jackdaw king when all the rest set upon the appointed king, stripped him of his borrowed plumes, and exposed him for the jackdaw that he was.

Awaiting the Match

All the ladies and gentlemen of the court were waiting in a special courtyard for the wrestling to begin. They wore many robes, one on top of another, heavy with embroidery and gold cloth, and sweat ran down their faces and froze in the winter afternoon. The gentlemen had long swords so weighted with gold and precious stones that they could never have used them, even if they had known how. The court ladies, their long black hair hanging down behind, had their faces painted dead white, which made them look frightened. They had pulled out their real eyebrows and painted new ones high above the place where eyebrows are supposed to be, and this made them all look as though they were very surprised at something.

Behind a screen sat the Emperor—by himself, because he was too noble for ordinary people to look at. He was a lonely old man with a kind, tired face. He hoped the wrestling would end quickly so he could go to his room and write poems.

Rating Cards for Primary Age Children

Very
Little
1

Little
2

Half&
Half
3

Much
4

Very
Much
5

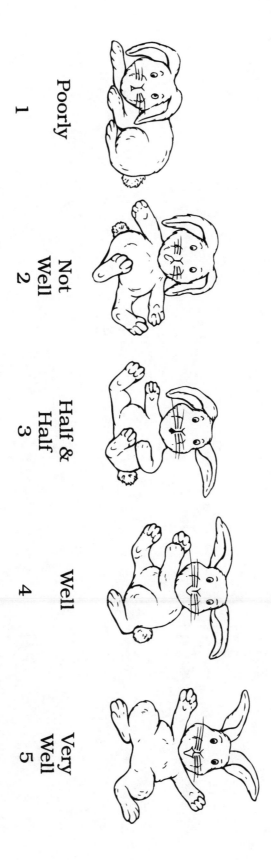

Poorly
1

Not
Well
2

Half &
Half
3

Well
4

Very
Well
5

Rating Cards for Intermediate Age Children

Very Little	Little	Half & Half	Much	Very Much
1	2	3	4	5

Poorly	Not Well	Half & Half	Well	Very Well
1	2	3	4	5

APPENDIX A: NO-CHARGE INVENTORIES AND LISTS*

Attitude Inventories

- Elementary Reading Attitude Survey. McKenna, M.C., & Kear, D.J. (1990). Measuring attitude toward reading: A new tool for teachers. *The Reading Teacher, 43,* 626–639.

- Estes, T.H., Estes, J.J., Richards, H.C., & Roettger, D. (1981). *Estes attitude scales: Measures of attitudes toward school subjects.* Austin, TX: Pro-Ed. (Out of print. One reproducible copy of scales plus manual available free from McGuffey Reading Center, 405 Emmet St., University of Virginia, Charlottesville, VA 22903; 804-924-3111.)

- George Incomplete Sentence Inventory. George, J.E. (1990). Course handout, University of Missouri—Kansas City, or copy from text. Manzo, A.V., & Manzo, U.C. (1993). *Literacy disorders: Holistic diagnosis and remediation.* Fort Worth, TX: Harcourt Brace, pp. 149–151. Note that permission from the publisher is needed to photocopy from the textbook.

Book Knowledge

- Checklist: Literary Appreciation—Establishing a Sense of Place and Time. Sharp, Quality Quinn (1989). *Evaluation: Whole language checklists for evaluating your children, for grades K to 6.* New York, NY: Scholastic, Inc., pp. 29–30.

- Checklist: Literary Appreciation—Recognizing Different Types of Literature. Sharp, Quality Quinn (1989). *Evaluation: Whole language checklists for evaluating your children, for grades K to 6.* New York, NY: Scholastic, Inc., pp. 35–36.

- Checklist: Literary Appreciation—Story Map Chart. Sharp, Quality Quinn (1989). *Evaluation: Whole language checklists for evaluating your children, for grades K to 6.* New York, NY: Scholastic, Inc., pp. 33–34.

- Checklist: Literary Appreciation—Understanding the Story's Characters. Sharp, Quality Quinn (1989). *Evaluation: Whole language checklists for evaluating your children, for grades K to 6.* New York, NY: Scholastic, Inc., pp. 31–32.

Comprehension

- Checklist: Cooperative Cloze Procedure. Sharp, Quality Quinn (1989). *Evaluation: Whole language checklists for evaluating your children, for grades K to 6.* New York, NY: Scholastic, Inc., p. 17.

- Checklist: Indicators for Valuing Oral Comprehension. Sharp, Quality Quinn (1989). *Evaluation: Whole language checklists for evaluating your children, for grades K to 6.* New York, NY: Scholastic, Inc., pp. 10–11.

- Checklist: Indicators for Valuing Reader Response. Sharp, Quality Quinn (1989). *Evaluation: Whole language checklists for evaluating your children, for grades K to 6.* New York, NY: Scholastic, Inc., pp. 15–16.

---

*To obtain other inventories and sources, write to A.V. Manzo, University of Missouri—Kansas City, 5100 Rockhill Road, Kansas City, MO 64110.

- Checklist: Indicators for Valuing Written Comprehension. Sharp, Quality Quinn (1989). *Evaluation: Whole language checklists for evaluating your children, for grades K to 6.* New York, NY: Scholastic, Inc., pp. 12–14.

- Checklist: Literary Appreciation—Story Map Chart. Sharp, Quality Quinn (1989). *Evaluation: Whole language checklists for evaluating your children, for grades K to 6.* New York, NY: Scholastic, Inc., pp. 33–34.

Cultural Differences

- Difference Inventory. Manzo, A.V., Meeks, (Hagar)J., & Eanet, M. Write A.V. Manzo, University of Missouri—Kansas City, 5100 Rockhill Road, Kansas City, MO 64110. Or copy from textbook: Manzo, A.V., & Manzo, U.C. (1993). *Literacy disorders: Holistic diagnosis and remediation.* Fort Worth, TX: Harcourt Brace, pp. 165–70. Note that permission from the publisher is needed to photocopy from the textbook.

Learning Styles Inventories

- Learning Preference Inventory. Write A.V. Manzo, University of Missouri—Kansas City, 5100 Rockhill Road, Kansas City, MO 64110. Or copy from textbook: Manzo, A.V., & Manzo, U.C. (1993). *Literacy disorders: Holistic diagnosis and remediation.* Fort Worth, TX: Harcourt Brace, pp. 158–64. Note that permission from the publisher is needed to photocopy from the textbook.

Metacognition and Study Skills

- Metacognition Strategy Index (MSI). Schmitt, M.C. (1990). A questionnaire to measure children's awareness of strategic reading processes. *The Reading Teacher*, 43(7), pp. 454–61. Or copy from textbook: Manzo, A.V., & Manzo, U.C. (1993). *Literacy disorders: Holistic diagnosis and remediation.* Fort Worth, TX: Harcourt Brace, pp. 117–22. Note that permission from the publisher is needed to photocopy from the textbook.

- Rogers' Study-Reading Skills Checklist. Rogers, D.B. (1984). Assessing study skills. *Journal of Reading*, 27(4), 346–54. Or copy from textbook: Manzo, A.V., & Manzo, U.C. (1993). *Literacy disorders: Holistic diagnosis and remediation.* Fort Worth, TX: Harcourt Brace, pp. 112–16. Note that permission from the publisher is needed to photocopy from the textbook.

Phonics/Letter Clusters/Word Lists

- 5 Frequency Counts of Occurrence of Phonic Elements. Copy from textbook: Manzo, A.V., & Manzo, U.C. (1993). *Literacy disorders: Holistic diagnosis and remediation.* Fort Worth, TX: Harcourt Brace, pp. 238–42. Note that permission from the publisher is needed to photocopy from the textbook.

- Predictable Phonic Rules. Copy from textbook: Manzo, A.V., & Manzo, U.C. (1993). *Literacy disorders: Holistic diagnosis and remediation.* Fort Worth, TX: Harcourt Brace, pp. 247–51. Note that permission from the publisher is needed to photocopy from the textbook.

- Letter Clusters—most frequent in first three levels of basals. Write Gerald G. Glass, Adelphi University, Garden City, NY 11530. Or copy from textbook: Manzo, A.V., & Manzo, U.C. (1993). *Literacy disorders: Holistic diagnosis and remediation.* Fort Worth, TX: Harcourt Brace, pp. 255. Note that permission from the publisher is needed to photocopy from the textbook.

- Checklist: Indicators for Valuing Miscue Analysis. Sharp, Quality Quinn (1989). *Evaluation: Whole language checklists for evaluating your children, for grades K to 6.* New York, NY: Scholastic, Inc., pp. 8–9.

Spelling

- Checklist: Spelling Analysis. Sharp, Quality Quinn (1989). *Evaluation: Whole language checklists for evaluating your children, for grades K to 6.* New York, NY: Scholastic, Inc., pp. 18–19.

Whole Language

- Checklist: Indicators for Valuing Early Reader Language Use Attempts. Sharp, Quality Quinn (1989). *Evaluation: Whole language checklists for evaluating your children, for grades K to 6.* New York, NY: Scholastic, Inc., pp. 5–7.

- Checklist: Student-As-Evaluator Ranking Chart. Sharp, Quality Quinn (1989). *Evaluation: Whole language checklists for evaluating your children, for grades K to 6.* New York, NY: Scholastic, Inc., pp. 26–28.

- Checklist: Teacher Anecdotal Record. Sharp, Quality Quinn (1989). *Evaluation: Whole language checklists for evaluating your children, for grades K to 6.* New York, NY: Scholastic, Inc., pp. 24–25.

Word Lists

- Dale-O'Rourke Vocabulary lists. In Dale, E., & O'Rourke, J. (1981). *The living word* (3rd ed.). Chicago: World Book-Childcraft International.

- Dolch Sight Words. Dolch, E.W. (1950), *Psychology of Reading.* Champaign, IL: Gerrard Press, p. 118.

- Eed's Core Words from Children's Literature. Eeds, M. (1985), *The Reading Teacher, 38,* pp. 412–23.

- Fry's "New Instant Word List." Fry, E. (1980), *The Reading Teacher, 34,* pp. 248–89.

- All of the above available in abridged forms in textbook: Manzo, A.V., & Manzo, U.C. (1993). *Literacy disorders: Holistic diagnosis and remediation.* Fort Worth, TX: Harcourt Brace.

Writing

- Checklist: Mechanics and Usage. Sharp, Quality Quinn (1989). *Evaluation: Whole language checklists for evaluating your children, for grades K to 6.* New York, NY: Scholastic, Inc., pp. 20–21.

- Checklist: Indicators for Valuing Writing Samples. Sharp, Quality Quinn (1989). *Evaluation: Whole language checklists for evaluating your children, for grades K to 6.* New York, NY: Scholastic, Inc., pp. 22–23.

- Checklist: Indicators for Valuing Written Comprehension. Sharp, Quality Quinn (1989). *Evaluation: Whole language checklists for evaluating your children, for grades K to 6.* New York, NY: Scholastic, Inc., pp. 12–14.

APPENDIX B: INFORMAL WRITING INVENTORY

Primer to Fourth Grade Level (also for upper grade students with more limited skills)

1. Have the student write out his or her own name and address (if able). Rank for:

	primitive	below average	average	above average	advanced
A. accuracy	1	2	3	4	5
B. legibility	1	2	3	4	5
C. spelling	1	2	3	4	5
D. placement on page (top left or center of page is best)	1	2	3	4	5
E. Comments _____					

2. Have the student speak or write a description of something that is pictured (see illustration). Record and rank for:

	primitive	below average	average	above average	advanced
A. accuracy (details)	1	2	3	4	5
B. reasonable sequence	1	2	3	4	5
C. cogency (lack of irrelevancies)	1	2	3	4	5
D. English usage	1	2	3	4	5
E. Comments _____					

3. Invite the student to complete several sentences (see examples). Record and rank for:

	primitive	below average	average	above average	advanced
A. relevancy	1	2	3	4	5
B. English usage	1	2	3	4	5
C. Comments _____					

Examples

1. Cats make me...

student response	relevancy	English usage
(a) sneeze and choke	5	4
(b) run	4	4

2. I wish that I could...

student response	relevancy	English usage
(a) go with my sister	4	3
(b) eat al thats I wanted	4	2

4. Have the student try to fill in a missing word from five sentences read to him. Record and rank for:

	primitive	below average	average	above average	advanced
A. accuracy (allow the student to change his or her mind)	1	2	3	4	5
B. syntax compatibility	1	2	3	4	5
C. semantics	1	2	3	4	5
D. prior knowledge	1	2	3	4	5
E. Comments _____					

Example

The cat and the _____ were chased off by the store owner.

Incorrect student answers and evaluations:

	"mouse"	"street"
accuracy	2	1
syntax compatibility	5	1
semantics	4	2
prior knowledge	4	2

---

5. Dictate two to five sentences, repeating each three times. Rate the student's transcription of the sentences for:

	primitive	below average	average	above average	advanced
A. accuracy	1	2	3	4	5
B. spelling and punctuation	1	2	3	4	5
C. penmanship	1	2	3	4	5
D. Comments _____					

6. Have a student tell you a story for two minutes. Offer the student three topic choices, and provide a minimum of ten minutes for the students to prepare for what they wish to say. Record the story told, and rate for:

	primitive	below average	average	above average	advanced
A. imagination	1	2	3	4	5
B. sequence	1	2	3	4	5
C. story form (beginning, middle, end)	1	2	3	4	5
D. internal logic (coherence)	1	2	3	4	5
E. overall quality	1	2	3	4	5
F. Comments _____					

7. Read or play back the story to the child, and ask what, if anything, they might like to revise. Limit the revision period to ten minutes. Make suggested revisions without unnecessary comments, and rate the revised story for:

	primitive	below average	average	above average	advanced
A. inclination to correct	1	2	3	4	5
B. quality of corrections	1	2	3	4	5

C. Comments _____

Fifth Grade to High School Level

1. Have students write a simple description (word translation) of a picture. Rate for:

	primitive	below average	average	above average	advanced
A. accuracy (details)	1	2	3	4	5
B. organization	1	2	3	4	5
C. usage/spelling/punctuation	1	2	3	4	5
D. overall	1	2	3	4	5
E. Comments _____					

2. Have students make up a four-to-eight-sentence discussion between a youngster and a mother as the youngster is about to leave the house. Rate for:

	primitive	below average	average	above average	advanced
A. imagination	1	2	3	4	5
B. sequence	1	2	3	4	5
C. usage/spelling/punctuation	1	2	3	4	5
D. overall	1	2	3	4	5
E. Comments _____					

3. Have students write a summary of a passage (250–500 words) at the student's independent to instructional reading level. Rate for:

	primitive	below average	average	above average	advanced
A. accuracy	1	2	3	4	5
B. sequence	1	2	3	4	5
C. absence of irrelevancies	1	2	3	4	5
D. usage/spelling/punctuation	1	2	3	4	5
E. Comments _____					

4. Have the student write a critical-evaluative piece on a topic, such as "What I think of vegetarians," or a reaction piece to a statement such as "There surely is life on neighboring planets." Rate for:

	primitive	below average	average	above average	advanced
A. maturity of judgement	1	2	3	4	5
B. accuracy of facts	1	2	3	4	5
C. usage/spelling/punctuation	1	2	3	4	5
D. overall	1	2	3	4	5
E. Comments _____					

Example
Name: Cindy
Grade: 7

Directions: Indicate whether you "totally disagree," "disagree," "partially agree," "agree," or "totally agree" with the statement that follows. Then explain why you feel as you do.

"There surely is life on neighboring planets."

I totally disagree with this because if there were(x) I think we would know about it by now. also the(x)cant possibly be any(x)because the planet in front of ours is too hot & the one behind ours is too cold.

Ratings
___

A. maturity of judgment	4
B. accuracy of facts	2
C. usage/spelling/punctuation	2
D. overall	3

E. Comments: Cindy shows some immature but basically sound scientific thinking. Punctuation needs some work.

5. Have student offer a constructive resolution to a problem, such as: "What can be done about the enormous amount of waste our society generates?" or "What can you do if someone decides to give you the silent treatment for no good reason?" Rate for:

	primitive	below average	average	above average	advanced
A. maturity	1	2	3	4	5
B. inventiveness	1	2	3	4	5
C. accuracy and relevance of facts	1	2	3	4	5
D. usage/spelling/punctuation	1	2	3	4	5
E. overall	1	2	3	4	5
F. Comments _____					

REFERENCES

Barr, R., Sadow, M., & Blachowicz, C. (1990). *Reading diagnosis for teachers: An instructional approach* (2nd ed.). White Plains, NY: Longman.

Baumann, J.F. (1988). *Reading assessment: An instructional decision-making perspective.* Columbus, OH: Merrill.

Betts, E.A. (l936). *The prevention and correction of reading difficulties.* Evanston, IL: Row Peterson.

Betts, E.A. (1946). *Foundations of reading instruction.* New York: American Book Co.

Byrne, B., & Fielding-Barnsley, R. (1991). Evaluation of a program to teach phonemic awareness to young children. *Journal of Educational Psychology, 83,* 451–55.

Cioffi, G., & Carney, J. J. (1983). Dynamic assessment of reading disabilities. *The Reading Teacher, 36,* 764–68.

Clark, H. (1977). Inferences in comprehension. In D. LaBerge & S.J. Samuels (eds.), Basic processes in reading: Perception and comprehension. Hillsdale, NJ: Lawrence Erlbaum.

Collins, C. (1991). Reading instruction that increases thinking abilities. *Journal of Reading, 34*(7), 510–16.

Cooter, R. B., & Flynt, E. S. (1986). *Reading comprehension: Out of the ivory tower and into the classroom.* Unpublished paper, Northwestern State University, Natchitoches, LA.

Dale, E. (1946). *The art of reading.* Ohio State University News Letter, 9, 1.

Dale, E., & O'Rourke, J. (1976). *The living word vocabulary.* Elgin, IL: Dome.

Dale, E., & O'Rourke, J. (1981). *The living word vocabulary* (3rd ed.). Chicago: World Book, Inc.

Dechant, E. (1981). *Diagnosis and remediation of reading disabilities.* Englewood Cliffs, NJ: Prentice Hall.

Eeds, M. (1985). Bookwords: Using a beginning word list of high frequency words from children's literature K–3. *The Reading Teacher, 38,* 418–23

Estes, T.H. (1991). In E. Fry (ed.), *Ten best ideas for reading teachers* (p. 59). New York: Addison Wesley.

Foorman, B.R., Francis, D.J., Novy, D.M., & Liberman, D. (1991). How letter-sound instruction mediates progress in first-grade reading and spelling. *Journal of Educational Psychology, 83,* 456–69.

Frederickson, C.H. (1975). Representing logical and semantic structure of knowledge acquired from discourse. *Cognitive Psychology, 7,* 371–458.

Fry, E.B. (1980). The new instant word list. *The Reading Teacher, 34,* 284–289.

Gomez, M.L., Graue, M.E., & Bloch, M.N. (1991). Reassessing portfolio assessment: Rhetoric and reality. *Language Arts, 68,* 620–28.

Goodman, K.S. (1973). Miscues: Windows on the reading process. In K. S. Goodman (ed.), *Miscue analysis: Applications to reading instruction* (pp. 3–14). Urbana, IL.: National Council of Teachers of English.

Haggard, M. (now Ruddell; 1976). *Creative Thinking-Reading Activities (CT-RA) as a means for improving comprehension.* Unpublished doctoral dissertation, University of Missouri—Kansas City, Kansas City, MO.

Halliday, M.A.K., & Hassan, R. (1976). *Cohesion in English.* London: Longman.

Holmes, B.C., & Roser, N.L. (1987). Five ways to assess readers' prior knowledge. *The Reading Teacher, 40,* 646–49.

Johns, J.L. (1977). Matching students with books. *Contemporary Education, 48,* 133–36.

Johns, J.L. (1988). Basic reading inventory (4th ed.). Dubuque, IA: Kendall/Hunt.

Johnson, D.D. (1971). A basic vocabulary for beginning reading. *Elementary School Journal, 72,* 29–34.

Johnson, M.S., Kress, R.A., & Pikulski, J.J. (1987). *Informal reading inventories* (2nd ed.). Newark, DE: IRA.

Johnston, P.H. (1983). *Reading comprehension assessment: A cognitive basis.* Newark, DE: IRA.

Kilgallon, P.A. (1942). A study of relationships among certain pupil adjustments in reading situations. Unpublished doctoral dissertation, Pennsylvania State College.

Kintsch, W., & van Dijk, T.A. (1978). Toward a model of text comprehension and production. *Psychological Review, 85,* 363–94.

LaPray, M., & Ross, R. (1969). The graded word list: Quick gauge of reading ability. *Journal of Reading, 12,* 305–307.

Leslie, L., & Caldwell, J. (1990). *Qualitative reading inventory.* Glenview, IL: Scott, Foresman.

Lipson, M.Y., & Wixson, K.K. (1991). *Assessment and instruction of reading disability: An interactive approach.* New York: HarperCollins.

McKenna, M.C. (1983). Informal reading inventories: A review of the issues. *The Reading Teacher, 36,* 670–79.

McKenna, M.C., & Layton, K. (1990). Concurrent validity of cloze as a measure of intersentential comprehension. *Journal of Educational Psychology, 82,* 372–77.

McKenna, M.C., & Robinson, R.D. (1993). *Teaching through text: A content literacy approach.* White Plains, NY: Longman.

Manzo, A.V. (1969). Improving reading comprehension through reciprocal questioning (Doctoral dissertation, Syracuse University, Syracuse, NY, 1968). *Dissertation Abstracts International, 30,* 5344A.

Manzo, A.V., & Manzo, U.C. (1993). *Literacy disorders: Holistic diagnosis and remediation.* New York: Harcourt Brace Jovanovich.

Manzo, A.V., & Manzo, U.C. (1994). *Teaching children to be literate: A reflective approach.* Fort Worth: Harcourt Brace.

Manzo, A.V., & McKenna, M.C. (April 1993). Factor structure of metacognition and related literacy variables. Paper presented at the meeting of the American Educational Research Association, Atlanta.

Nicholson, T. (1991). Do children read words better in context or in lists? A classic study revisited. *Journal of Educational Psychology, 83,* 444–50.

Olson, M.W., & Gillis, M.K. (1987). Text type and text structure: An analysis of three secondary informal reading inventories. *Reading Horizons, 28,* 70–80.

Paratore, J.R., & Indrisano, R. (1987). Intervention assessment of reading comprehension. *Reading Teacher, 40,* 778–83.

Paris, S.G., & Myers, M. (1981). Comprehension monitoring, memory and study strategies of good and poor readers. *Journal of Reading Behavior, 13,* 5–22.

Pearson, P.D., Hansen, J., & Gordon, C. (1979). The effect of background knowledge on young children's comprehension of explicit and implicit information. *Journal of Reading Behavior, 11,* 201–09.

Peters, C.W., & Wixson, K.K. (1989). Smart new reading tests are coming. *Learning, 17(8),* 43–44, 53.

Pikulski, J.J., & Shanahan, T. (1982). Informal reading inventories: A critical analysis. In J.J. Pikulski & T. Shanahan (eds.), *Approaches to the informal evaluation of reading,* pp. 94–116. Newark, DE: IRA.

Powell, W.R. (1970). Reappraising the criteria for interpreting informal inventories. In D.L. DeBoer (ed.), *Reading diagnosis and evaluation: IRA conference proceedings* (vol. 13, part 4), pp. 100–109. Newark, DE: IRA.

Powell, W.R. (1971). The validity of the instructional reading level. In R.L. Leibert (ed.), *Diagnostic viewpoints in reading: IRA conference proceedings* (vol. 15), pp. 121–33. Newark, DE: IRA.

Powell, W.R., & Dunkeld, C.G. (1971). Validity of the IRI reading levels. *Elementary English, 48,* 637–42.

Ratanakarn, S. (1992). A comparison of reader classification by traditional text-dependent measures and by addition of text-independent measures. Doctoral dissertation, University of Missouri—Kansas City.

Rayner, K., & Pollatsek, A. (1989). *The psychology of reading.* Englewood Cliffs, NJ: Prentice Hall.

Recht, D.R., & Leslie, L. (1988). The effect of prior knowledge on good and poor readers' memory for text. *Journal of Educational Psychology, 80,* 16–20.

Schatz, E.K., & Baldwin, R.S. (1986). Context clues are unreliable predictors of word meanings. *Reading Research Quarterly, 21,* 439–53.

Schell, L.M., & Hanna, G.S. (1981). Can informal reading inventories reveal strengths and weaknesses in comprehension subskills? *The Reading Teacher, 35,* 263–68.

Searles, E.F. (1988). What's the value of an IRI? Is it being used? *Reading Horizons, 28,* 92–101.

Shanahan, T., Kamil, M.L., & Tobin, A.W. (1982). Cloze as a measure of intersentential comprehension. *Reading Research Quarterly, 17,* 229–55.

Silvaroli, N.J. (1990). Classroom reading inventory (6th ed.). Dubuque, IA: William C. Brown.

Smith, F. (1988). *Understanding reading: A psycholinguistic analysis of reading and learning to read* (4th ed.). Hillsdale, NJ: Lawrence Erlbaum.

Stanovich, K.E. (1991). Word recognition: Changing perspectives. In R. Barr, M.L. Kamil, P. B. Mosenthal, & P. D. Pearson (eds.), *Handbook of reading research* (vol. 2), pp. 418–52. White Plains, NY: Longman.

Stauffer, R.G. (1969). *Directing reading maturity as a cognitive process.* New York: Harper & Row.

Thorndike, E.L. (1917). Reading as reasoning: A study of mistakes in paragraph reading. *Journal of Educational Psychology, 8,* 323–32.

Vellutino, F.R. (1991). Introduction to three studies on reading acquisition: Convergent findings on theoretical foundations of code-oriented versus whole-language approaches to reading instruction. *Journal of Educational Psychology, 83,* 437–43.

Zakaluk, B.L., & Samuels, S.J. (1988). Toward a new approach to predicting text comprehensibility. In B.L. Zakaluk & S.J. Samuels (eds.), *Readability: Its past, present, and future,* pp. 121–44. Newark, DE: IRA.

INDEX